Curious
CAMDEN TOWN

Curious Camden Town
by Martin Plaut and Andrew Whitehead

Published in 2015
by Five Leaves Publications, www.fiveleaves.co.uk

Copyright (c) Martin Plaut and Andrew Whitehead
ISBN: 978-1-010170-23-6
Design by Chris Matthews
Printed and bound in Great Britain

Curious
CAMDEN TOWN

Martin Plaut and Andrew Whitehead

FIVE LEAVES PUBLICATIONS
www.fiveleaves.co.uk

CONTENTS

Introduction 7

1. Revolution at the Roundhouse 10
2. Amy Winehouse's Camden 15
3. Arlington House 19
4. Tom Sayers – the 'Little Wonder' 23
5. 'Modernism for Suburbia' 27
6. Burlesque at the Black Cap 29
7. The Belgian connection 33
8. The Johnny Cash cash machine 36
9. The mystery of the Regent's Park Barracks 38
10. Blair's funeral 41
11. Vinot Cars 45
12. Morris On 50
13. The Cumberland Market Group 52
14. 'Dig for Victory' 55
15. The cat goddesses 59
16. Richard Cobden – unknown hero 65
17. A black revolutionary 68
18. The Working Men's College – fading away 72
19. The shadow of a shadow 74
20. A movement that shook the world 78
21. The final chord 81
22. St Martin's Almshouses 83
23. The EOKA priest 86
24. Lawford's Wharves 92
25. The Camden Town Murder 93
26. The eternal optimists 96
27. Sherlock's temple 99
28. École de Pole 101
29. Eels, Pie and Mash 103

INTRODUCTION

Camden Town is a very lived-in part of London – and it has lustre too. A global reputation, a diverse local community, a wonderful place to walk around.

Some of the people and places which make Camden renowned, from Amy Winehouse to the Roundhouse, feature in these pages. But so do lots of localities, buildings, foundation stones and faded street art which even locals may not know about. The stories attached to them – about prize fighters, Morris dancers, drag queens and pole dancers – are even more extraordinary.

If you are local to Camden Town (as we are) and love the place (as we do), we hope *Curious Camden Town* will help you see the area anew. If you are exploring from afar, this will take you to some of the nooks and crannies which don't feature in the guide books, and will give you much more of a sense of the place and its people. It's an edgy neighbourhood, at times troubled as so many inner city areas are, but with warmth and energy and well worth getting to know.

This book is no history: as with our previous publication *Curious Kentish Town*, it is an eclectic assemblage of places and people, moments and monuments, that captured our interest. We make no apology for the selection – there is much of merit that we have missed out, but then Camden is overflowing with the remarkable, the inspiring and, yes, the tragic too.

This is a celebration of Camden Town, in all its complexity – we invite you to join us on our tour. There's a map should you wish to follow in our footsteps. And if you relish the photos and enjoy the stories, we're quite sure you will want to savour these spots for yourselves.

Martin Plaut and Andrew Whitehead

1 | REVOLUTION AT THE ROUNDHOUSE

It all happened in an engine shed. If there was a time and place when Camden Town became cool, it was at the Roundhouse one October evening in 1966. That was the moment when psychedelia came into style and Camden gained the counter-culture credentials which, in very different fashion, are still reflected in the trendy stalls and markets around Camden Lock. The venue for that political, musical, cultural conjuncture was, fittingly perhaps, a legacy of the defining aspect of the old, soot-ridden Camden: the railways.

The construction of the main rail lines turned early Victorian Camden Town upside down carving a huge swathe through the area. Charles Dickens's *Dombey and Son*, published in the second-half of the 1840s, took as one of its themes the intrusion of the railways into a part of London he knew well. It was, he wrote, 'a great earthquake':

> *Houses were knocked down; streets broken through and stopped; deep pits and trenches dug in the ground … In short, the yet unfinished and unopened Railroad was in progress; and, from the very core of all this dire disorder, trailed smoothly away, upon its mighty course of civilisation and improvement.*

It sounds like HS2!

Just as *Dombey and Son* was appearing in serialised form, detailing the devastation visited on Camden's fictional Stagg's Gardens, the Roundhouse was being built as a locomotive shed, complete with a turntable which gave this glorious building its name and shape. That turntable was only used for about a decade, because the engines got too big. The building then became a warehouse, notably for Gilbey's gin, and eventually fell derelict.

The renaissance of the Roundhouse started in 1964 when the playwright Arnold Wesker launched Centre 42 there, winning trade union support for the creation of an arts and

cultural centre. But the moment that Camden became hip was two years later, on 15th October 1966 – when Pink Floyd and Soft Machine, neither then signed up to a record label, played at the all-night launch party of *International Times* (*IT*), one of the more cerebral of the ventures of the sixties alternative press.

It was the first big gig ever held at the Roundhouse. The building wasn't remotely fit for purpose, as Barry Miles, a founder of *IT*, recalled in his history of the city's counter-culture, *London Calling*:

> *there was no proper floor, and great jagged pieces of metal stuck up through a layer of grime. There were only two toilets, and the electricity supply was about the same as that of a small house, powerful enough only to light the building. There were several large doors opening out on to the railway freight yards, but the entrance staircase from Chalk Farm Road was so narrow that only one person at a time could enter or leave.*

On that night, 2,000 youngsters made their way up and down that far-from-adequate stairwell.

But the venue delivered. "It was great," recalls top record producer Joe Boyd. "Very raw, dirt on the floor, unheated – but strangely spectacular."

The 'shortest/barest' contest – what a stark reminder of the sexist side of psychedelia – was won, Miles recalls, by Marianne Faithfull, 'for an extremely abbreviated nun's outfit'. Mini-skirted women handed out lumps of sugar – they weren't laced with LSD but some went on a trip all the same. A motorcycle weaved in and out of the audience, revving in sync with the music. A reveller made eye-catching shapes in the air with a sparkler – Adam Ritchie was at the Roundhouse that night taking photographs, and he regards 'Sparklerman' as best capturing the mood of that remarkable moment.

Then there was a giant green jelly which was intended to be part of the performance. But as it was tipped out of a tea chest, the jelly snagged on the rim and spilt and slithered all

ALL NIGHT RAVE to launch new underground newspaper 'INTERNATIONAL TIMES'; the Soft Machine; the Pink Floyd; Steel Bands

STRIP – TRIPS – HAPPENING
MOVIE – POP – OP – COSTUME
MASQUE – DRAG BALL

bring your own poison, bring Flowers & Gass filled balloons

surPRIZE for Shortest & Barest

at... **THE ROUND HOUSE** *
opp. chalk farm underground

SAT. 15th OCT 11 P.M. onwards.

advance tickets 5/- from INDICA books; Dobells Record Shop; better books; Mandarin Book Shops at... **GRANNIE TAKE A TRIP** Nottinghill gate & Swiss Cottage, or compulsory donations of **10/-** at door over the floor. "So I took off my clothes and jumped in," recalls Mike Lesser, still associated with the now online *International Times*. A photographer was at hand – an image which he has been unable to escape. "Me standing up stark bollock naked in the jelly – it's haunted my life!"

And on the stage? 'The Pink Floyd, psychedelic pop group,' – reported *IT* in its second issue – 'did weird things to the feel of the event with … slide projections playing on their skin … spotlights flashing in time with the drums.' It was one of the first psychedelic light shows. The fuses finally blew at the end of the Floyd's Interstellar Overdrive.

Dianne Lifton, then a 21-year-old fashion designer, is fairly sure she was at the *IT* launch – but then, as folks say, if you can remember it, you weren't there. "I was rebellious, up for anything and living in Camden Town. It wasn't yet one of the key locations of swinging London that it was destined to be in a year or so, but it was the time of Arts Laboratories and experimental happenings, and the Roundhouse was one of the alternative venues we used."

She has a clearer recall of the New Year's Eve event of 'psyche-kinetic destruction' at the Roundhouse a few weeks later, with an even more stellar line-up. A press release promised that The Who, 'pioneers of destructive pop', would 'attack their array of electronic gear', while The Move would 'get through TV sets etc' and Pink Floyd promised light effects to match.

While the bands played, Di and a friend – at the behest of an artist – drove a silver-sprayed Cadillac into the auditorium. "I was both excited and terrified" – the terror coming from driving into crowds who were facing the other way, standing and dancing near the stage. "We were both dressed from head to foot in silver – soft helmets, in vogue at the time, silver mini culottes" – she still has these – "and silver tights. Bringing the car to a standstill at the foot of the stage, we both got out carrying large axes and began to smash the car. Friends standing round us were unable to hold back the crowds, some of whom wanted to stop us while others wanted to help and grabbed the axes from us." Smashing!

The Roundhouse quickly became the counter-culture's venue of choice. Two years later its bookshop of choice, Compendium, opened a short distance away on Camden High Street, selling beat poetry, obscure anarchist papers and a lot more to supply the scene. It remained there until 2000 when the shop became – ouch! – a Dr Martens. A Sunday crafts market got going at Camden Lock in the early seventies. That developed, for good or ill, into the Camden market scene of today.

What a transformation. As Barry Miles has said, 'that whole area was just bleak and dead before the Roundhouse became a venue'. The loos are better, and the stairs a whole load safer, at the Roundhouse these days – and happily it continues to be a great place for music and performance.

2 | AMY WINEHOUSE'S CAMDEN

As the light begins to fade and a cold drizzle falls, Camden can seem a very different place. Music pumps out of the many venues, neon lights flash and on the pavements young men offer a range of substances.

Sleazy, edgy, different, enticing: it's the place your mother doesn't want you to go. No wonder a young North Londoner like Amy Winehouse found it so inviting. "I feel I can do anything I want in Camden. It's like my playground," she told her father, Mitch, in July 2011. Nine days later she was dead.

If there was just one venue that was associated with Amy, it was the Hawley Arms, right next to Camden Lock on Castlehaven Road. This was the pub that Amy made her own; it's where she would come to relax and be herself. Dealing with fame became increasingly difficult for her. The attention was so intense and it was difficult for her to just turn up at the pub and behave as she wished, although she tried.

Piers Hernu, a journalist who knew her well, described how she could play in front of 60,000 people and then come into the Hawley Arms to serve behind the bar. 'She would be in

here, and much happier, pulling pints the next night.' Locals remember her as loud, proud and in your face.

The Camden that Amy knew and loved stretched from the Roundhouse, where she made her final public appearance on 20th July 2011. She took to the stage for one last time supporting her godchild, the 15-year-old soul singer Dionne Bromfield, singing 'Mama Said' with The Wanted. It went via her main hangouts in Camden Town and on to the Euston Road and University College Hospital.

It was there, at 1am on 7th August 2007, that her partner (and husband of two years) Blake Fielder-Civil dragged Amy through the doors to the A&E department. They gave her adrenaline and pumped her stomach. She admitted taking cocaine, booze and marijuana. *The Sun* carried a headline:

'Amy's 3-Day Binge: Coke, Ecstasy, Horse tranquiliser, Vodka, Whiskey.' It was the kind of publicity that was to follow her to her death four years later, at the age of just 27. It was not the last occasion on which UCH would be called on to resuscitate her.

Amy's first home of her own was in East Finchley, when she moved into a flat with her best friend, Juliette Ashby, in 2002 at the age of 19. The flat-mates had known each other since they met at primary school, aged four. The flat on Leopold Road was purchased with Amy's first advance from EMI – a colossal £73,437.50. Soon the girls were smoking dope and enjoying the buzz of the area: "I've got such brilliant memories of that flat," recalls Juliette. "I'd have passed out from being stoned and Amy would be roasting a chicken at three in the morning."

But Camden was the place where Amy felt most at home. She blended in perfectly with her winkle-pickers, piercings and tattoos – and later her large, sassy beehive. For many years Amy was – and wanted to be – just another local character. She would cruise the streets, buying records from the Oxfam shop in Kentish Town and playing at tiny venues like the Dublin Castle on Parkway.

Amy had a reputation as a fine pool player, dropping in on the Good Mixer on Inverness Street and whipping everyone in sight. She was to continue coming even after she had achieved fame – only with a minder or two in tow. And it was here that Amy, now 21, came across Blake Fielder-Civil, a part-time gofer in the music-video business.

Her mother, Janis, says that Amy loved to recount how they met. "I walked into the pub, strolled over to the pool table and there he was. I knew he's seen me out of the corner of his eye. I took the pool cue and played him. I wiped him out."

Immediately attracted to each other, it was the relationship with Blake that would finally destroy her. Blake admitted introducing Amy to heroin, although her family today accept that she was as responsible for their drug habits as he was.

Fame also brought isolation. 'She couldn't do what she loved which was bouncing around Camden talking to everyone. She was bored and she was lonely,' Hernu told the *Guardian* after her death.

Amy attempted rehab many times, immortalised in her well-known song of the same name, which she brought out in October 2006. She tried other strategies, including joining the all-woman gym Fitness First on Albert Street. She knuckled down to a strict regime for a while, but it didn't last.

In 2008 Amy bought a new home, this time a quaint enclave, tucked away from the bustle of Camden Town. Purchased at a cost of £260,000, it was at 25 Prowse Place, close to Camden Road station and the North London line. It could have been something of a sanctuary for her. But soon her fans and the paparazzi found out and began camping out in the street. Neighbours complained that they were being kept awake by the incessant noise of cars and the flash of cameras going off. The photographers would relieve themselves in the bushes, much to the distaste of the locals.

Less than a year before her death, Amy's father, Mitch, bought a property on Camden Square as a place to which she

could escape. The £1.8 million house with its three double bedrooms, three reception rooms and an ample rear garden could have been a real home for his daughter.

But, like other attempts to save or reform the singer, 30 Camden Square didn't work. She soon relapsed into booze and drugs. After her death the area became for a time a shrine for fans, who came in their hundreds. Flowers were left, local street signs removed.

Her life has been captured in a raw and unflattering documentary, *Amy*, drawing on early home films and complemented by interviews with her friends and fans, all intercut with her irresistible singing. It is uncompromising about her father, and unsurprisingly, Mitch hated the film. It has been a box office success: one of the highest earning British documentaries.

In September 2014 Camden finally gave Amy a permanent memorial. A statue of the lanky, defiant young woman stands in the Stables Market at Camden Lock. Unveiling the statue, the actress Barbara Windsor described her as 'one of the greatest talents this country has ever produced…a warm, lovely, kind and fun lady.'

Her fans still come, to be photographed, lay flowers and shed a tear by the statue. Would Amy have approved of the adulation? We shall never know.

3 | ARLINGTON HOUSE

Arlington House, just around the corner from Camden Lock, was once one of Camden's most important institutions. Built in 1905 it provided generations of poor, working class men, with decent, affordable accommodation.

This workingmen's hostel was constructed for Montagu William Lowry-Corry, better known as Lord Rowton (1838 – 1903). A Conservative politician, he rose to run the navy (as First Lord of the Admiralty) and became private secretary to the prime minister, Benjamin Disraeli. But today he is best known as a philanthropist, building the hostels which became

known as 'Rowton Houses'. There were once six of them in London; only Arlington House remains in use as a hostel.

Many made these hostels their home. Joseph Stalin stayed at one in Whitechapel for a fortnight in 1907. George Orwell wrote about living in one of the houses in *Down and Out in Paris and London*:

> *The best [lodging houses] are the Rowton Houses, where the charge is a shilling, for which you get a cubicle to yourself, and the use of excellent bathrooms. You can also pay half a crown for a special, which is practically hotel accommodation. The Rowton Houses are splendid buildings, and the only objection to them is the strict discipline, with rules against cooking, card playing, etc*

Arlington House was the largest and best known of these lodgings. The writer Brendan Behan was just one of many Irishmen who found a place to stay here.

As Orwell said, discipline was strict. Danny lived in Arlington House in the 1970s, and his memories of that time were recorded by the Irish Tenants' Association:

> *You had to be out of your bed by nine o'clock in the morning. If you came down late three days in a row...three times and you were OUT. They had a guy called Albert, who locked up, and he checked those who came down late... The majority of the people in Arlington House at that time worked and paid their own rent. Nobody signed on, or was interested in it. There was 1,140 rooms; 140 staff, 1000 men.*

The accommodation was spartan but clean and some men lived in Arlington House for years. But by the 1980s conditions had deteriorated badly. Robert Latham, chairman of Camden's Labour-controlled housing committee, said that 777 of the 1,066 rooms were just thirty-five square feet in size, and half the minimum required by public health standards. The staff were also poorly treated – taking home just £26 for a 48 hour week. 'The living conditions are bad,' he complained. 'It is certainly not a hostel that is suitable for the 1980s.'

In 1982 a dispute led to the management attempting to evict the staff. It took intervention by the Camden Labour Party, a late night ruling by a judge in chambers and the rather sceptical involvement of the police to prevent the forty strikers from being thrown out.

In the end the council intervened, taking over Arlington House before passing it over to the One Housing Group. A major refurbishment later, it now provides ninety-five private units for the homeless. Although these are still small, they do have private showers and toilets. In addition there are forty-four cheap studio flats for young workers with a connection to Camden. There is a strong demand for the facilities. "We never have voids," says Dilek Karatas, from the management team. In addition there are training facilities in catering, building and the arts and a substantial conference centre.

The building today is bright, modern and busy. It is a far cry from the days when Arlington House was home to the Irish poor who came to London in search of work – digging the canals and building the underground on which the capital still depends.

4 | TOM SAYERS - THE 'LITTLE WONDER'

As you jostle the crowds on your way from Camden tube to the Lock, past the buskers, chuggers and tourists, pause for a moment and look up at number 257. There, high above a shop selling sweatshirts and cheap sunglasses, is a blue plaque which reads: 'Tom Sayers 1826-1865 Pugilist died here'.

Who would believe that this simple memorial commemorates one of England's greatest sporting heroes – and certainly one of its bravest?

Tom Sayers was a prize-fighter: a bare knuckle boxer who fought before the sport was regulated. Punches were exchanged

for hours, until one of the contestants could take it no more. The fights were illegal, yet Sayers's exploits were followed avidly across the nation. Even Queen Victoria asked to be kept informed.

Sayers also participated in the very first international heavyweight championship match. This pitted the 5'8" Sayers (sometimes known as the 'Napoleon of the Prize Ring') against a much taller opponent, the 6' 2" John C. Heenan of the United States; but more of that later.

Tom Sayers was born into a poor family in Brighton – the youngest of five children. He had little education and was almost illiterate. At the age of thirteen he went to London, to become a bricklayer. Sayers worked on many sites, including the construction of King's Cross Station. He lived in a notorious slum just north of King's Cross – Agar Town, a name that lives on in Agar Grove (earlier called St Paul's Road).

Prize fighting had been illegal in Britain since the middle of the eighteenth century, but the sport continued underground. Sayers decided to try his luck in March 1849, defeating Abe Couch. In 1853, after three more victories, he took on the middleweight champion, Nat Langham. The fight – over sixty rounds – lasted for just over two hours. It was Sayers's only defeat.

Long though that bout was, it was not the fighter's longest. That took place in 1857, when he defeated Harry Paulson in three hours eight minutes – a contest of 109 rounds! His prowess earned him the nicknames of the 'Little Wonder'.

In 1859 Sayers was challenged by the American champion, John Heenan. 'Dear Sir,' Sayers replied, 'I aksep yor Chalang tue fite without gloves oktuber 24. Yrs. truly Thomas Sayers. staiks £500 a side, J.C. Heenan Esq.'

And so the two men met on the morning of 17th April 1860 in a field at Farnborough in Hampshire. The fight attracted attention on both sides of the Atlantic. The *New York Clipper* reported: '"Whate'er we do, where'er we be," fight, fight, fight is the topic that engrosses all attention.' *The Times* put things more directly: 'Much as all decent people disliked the idea of two fine men meeting to beat each other half to death, it was nevertheless devoutly wished that, as somebody was to be beaten, it might be the American.'

Vast crowds gathered at Waterloo station to catch southbound 'specials'. Three-guinea tickets were stamped 'To Nowhere'. The newly formed Metropolitan Police had men dotted along the track to try to prevent the contest. Despite this many in high society made the journey, including – reportedly – Charles Dickens, W.M. Thackeray and the 19-year-old Prince of Wales. Suggestions that the prime minister, Lord Palmerston, was in attendance are – apparently – incorrect.

The contest – the first of many deemed the 'fight of the century' – was a bloody affair. Heenan towered above his British opponent. After more than forty rounds Sayers's right arm was injured and Heenan's right eye closed. At this point Heenan managed to grab Sayers. An eye-witness, Henry J. Coke, recorded what happened next:

> [Heenan] forced Sayers' neck on to the rope, and, with all his weight, leant upon the Englishman's shoulders. In a few moments the face of the strangled man was black, his tongue was forced out of his mouth, and his eyes from their sockets. His arms fell powerless, and in a second or two more he would have been a corpse.
> With a wild yell the crowd rushed to the rescue. Warning cries of 'the police, the police' mingled with the shouts. The ropes were cut, and a scamper for the waiting train ended this last of the greatest prize-fights.

Sayers, although badly hurt, managed to recover sufficiently to quaff champagne at The Swan on the Old Kent Road. Heenan was in a critical condition for 48 hours, recovering in a totally darkened room.

In the event the fight was declared a draw with both men being awarded the prize – though many Americans believed their man had been cheated of victory. A public subscription raised £3,000 for Sayers, on condition he retire. And this he did.

Sayers went into the circus business. He lived at 257 Camden High Street with his friend, the boot maker, John Mensley. He was a popular hero, travelling in a carriage, with his faithful dog Lion at his feet.

Sayers died on November 8th 1865 and thousands – tens of thousands, if you believe some accounts – attended his funeral. He was buried at Highgate West Cemetery. The crowd following the coffin was distinctly rowdy. They were said to have 'danced and screamed, yelled and hooted, whistled and shrieked, like demons…' for the hero they loved. They swarmed over the cemetery, damaging tombs and breaking branches.

Today Sayers's modest tombstone can be seen in the cemetery – his trusty hound Lion, faithful to the end, depicted in stone at the foot of his master's grave.

5 | 'MODERNISM FOR SUBURBIA'

You get the best view of Bowman's and its marvelous mosaics from the top deck of the bus going up Camden High Street. Look right a bit beyond the Post Office and there they are above the first-floor windows – not large or showy, but very tasteful. They advertise the range of wares that this 'progressive' household store once sold – Drapery, Curtains, Furniture, Carpets, Bedsteads, Bedding. There's also a locomotive engine and, more incongruously, a ship with sail and curved prow which appears to date from the Phoenician era.

Look a little higher up, and there are more mosaic designs above the second floor windows. These continue on the northern aspect of the building on Greenland Street. And if you hop off the bus and admire the Bowman's building from the other side of Camden High Street, with its clock (stuck at two o'clock), Arts and Crafts-style chimney, gables and dauntingly steep roof, you are looking at the architectural highlight at the heart of Camden Town, a locality repeatedly described by

the rather sniffy Pevsner, in his multi-volume bible of London architecture, as 'scruffy'.

This was for ninety years Camden Town's smartest store. The Bowman brothers set up as upholsterers on the high street in the 1860s, and transformed themselves over the years into the 'complete house furnishers'.

The shop which now is such an unremarked upon jewel of our area was purpose-built in 1893, replacing premises damaged by fire. You can tell from the ambition of the design, and the size of the store, that there was money around in Camden in those days. And Bowman's once extended into the adjoining building behind – Denmoss House, which fronts Greenland Street – which still bears bold 'BOWMAN BROS' signage. Perhaps this was where some of the furniture was made.

Bowman Brothers developed a deserved reputation as 'progressive' furnishers – selling stylish, quality pieces for the increasingly prosperous north London suburbs: 'the first firm to sell good modern designs at reasonable prices', it boasted.

Bowman's catalogues from the inter-war years were every bit as smart as their sofas and bedroom suites – and they are eagerly collected. Top commercial artists were commissioned to design the catalogue covers, there was a touch of mischief and humour throughout and the furniture had that ring of aspiration which appealed to the middle class.

Bowman's 'were keen to promote ideals of good design and fitness for purpose, based on teaching of the Bauhaus in Germany, amongst others', says the Museum of Domestic Design and Architecture at Middlesex University. 'Bowmans' furniture was modernism for suburbia … softened around its edges for a mass market.' And to this day, the Bowman's label on a piece of second-hand furniture adds a premium to the price.

The store kept going as a family business until 1971, and seems finally to have closed in 1982. Bowman's is now a distant memory, and the spot is currently taken by an unholy trinity of Burger King, Poundland and Waterstones. But the building remains in good repair, and those mosaics are a continuing reminder of the Camelot that once was Camden High Street.

6 | BURLESQUE AT THE BLACK CAP

This was a demonstration that had it all: noisy, boisterous – with not a hint of funereal gloom. The Black Cap, Camden's premier gay bar, had closed on 12th April 2015. Drag queens, patrons, activists and local well-wishers came together outside the pub to protest against the decision to bring this iconic venue to an end. The owners, Faucet Inns, plan to transform it into flats.

Meth, one of the performers at the bar, said the staff had been told on a Friday that it was closing on Sunday. "We had a gagging order slapped on us by the company – with threats that staff would not be able to find jobs if we went public. They told us not to tell people; we told as many people as we could to make sure we still had a fair amount of people to say goodbye to her on Sunday."

"It was where I grew up, where I learnt my trade," said John Moore (stage name Mrs Moore). "It has a great history. In August 2013 we celebrated fifty years of the Black Cap as a gay venue. It always had real people in it – it was never pretentious!"

The pub itself can trace its roots back much further. A list of inns in Camden from about 1830 includes the 'Mother Black Cap,' and it may date from even earlier. High on the frontage is a bust of a rather prim looking woman which is said to be a representation of a 17th century witch, which gave the pub its name. But by the 1960s it had become a gay meeting place and gradually gained a reputation for drag.

Among the earliest performers was Mrs Shufflewick, aka Rex Jameson. Night after night she would appear, a tipsy cockney woman settled in the snug of her local pub, The Cock & Comfort: 'A lot of comfort, but not much of anything else.' Mrs Shufflewick drank her port and lemon, seated primly in her flowery hat and shabby fur stole, with her 'genuine untouched pussy', as an obituary put it.

Rex Jameson learnt his trade when he was called up for war service in 1942. He joined the RAF Gang Show, which starred comedians Peter Sellers, Frankie Howerd and Spike Milligan. Rex really came into his own after the war, performing on television and at Blackpool's Winter Gardens. But the Black Cap became his performing home and it was after a show here that he died in 1983.

Father Bernard Lynch, who today chairs the Camden LGBT Forum, remembers arriving from New York in 1992 and walking into the Black Cap. "It was outrageous," he recalls. "I had seen nothing like it before." But it was an easy place to make friends. Among those he met was Reginald Bundy – the drag queen Regina Fong - who titled herself: 'Her Imperial Highness: The last of the Romanovs'. Lynch, a Catholic priest, presided at Bundy's funeral.

The pub became known as the Palladium of drag. Danny La Rue and Hinge and Bracket started their careers here. "These men were our revolutionaries," says Lynch. "They were always out there, to be laughed with and to be laughed at."

The Black Cap also served an important function. "It was a place of sanctuary – and an important one, right to the end," says Lynch. "People knew they would be defended if they were attacked – which still happens."

But, says Moore, the pub also had a darker edge. "The serial killer, Dennis Nilsen, picked up some of his victims here. People remembered." Carl Stottor, a 21-year-old who met Nilsen in the Black Cap, was one of at least twelve men murdered at Nilsen's home on Cranley Gardens by the man dubbed in the press as 'the Muswell Hill murderer'.

In recent years the venue suffered a slow, but gradual decline. "The gay lifestyle became normalised, and people became integrated into London life," Lynch reflects. "Audiences dwindled. Fifteen years ago it was busy seven nights a week, open until 2am." By the end it was really only full at weekends.

John Moore sees the Black Cap's fate differently. "There was no investment. The toilets were in a shocking state. Even bulbs to light the stage were not replaced." He believes it was a deliberate strategy to run down the venue.

"I doubt it will re-open. But power to the people!" says John, more in hope than expectation.

Since we met the pub has had its status as an 'Asset of Community Value' upheld. But the landlords might still appeal. Will the Black Cap return to its former glory? No one can be certain.

7 | THE BELGIAN CONNECTION

What was the largest single influx of refugees into Britain? You'll never get it (unless you've read the title to these paragraphs). A quarter-of-a-million Belgians came over to Britain when their country was invaded by Germany during the First World War. They set up their own schools, newspapers, hospitals, shops – there were even Belgian 'colonies' in England run by the Belgian government and using Belgian currency.

For such a huge exodus, it has left little mark. Almost all the refugees returned to Belgium within a year of the war ending. But in Camden, a small number of Belgian priests stayed – eventually founding the Catholic church on Arlington Road which is still named after a Belgian shrine, Our Lady of Hal.

During the war, the Scheut fathers, a Belgian missionary order, decided to move their base to London lock, stock and barrel. Within a few years, they sought to establish a church, with the dual purpose of providing a spiritual focus for the Belgian Catholic community across the capital and serving a locality which had no Catholic church close at hand. The initial building on Arlington Road opened in 1922. It was little more than a hut, opposite where the church now stands, and almost from the start proved insufficient to accommodate the congregation, which was in large part of Irish origin.

The current church was completed in 1933. The architectural style is said to be based on traditional Flemish design. It's certainly a better than average inter-war church and greatly loved by those who worship there.

The Arlington Road entrance doesn't immediately catch the eye – though there's a charming mosaic as well as inscriptions which explain the Belgian connection. A small side chapel, the Hal chapel – usually open for an hour or so after midday mass – has a likeness of Our Lady in dark wood, a replica of the venerated medieval statue at Hal (or Halle) outside Brussels. Also in the chapel is a panel bearing a profile of King Albert of the Belgians, the country's sovereign through the First World War who died in a mountaineering accident in 1934. The work was commissioned in his memory by 'the Belgian colony in Great Britain', though by the time it was finished the country was again caught up in a world war.

The Scheut fathers ran the church into the 1980s when it was handed over to the diocese and all but one of the Belgian priests returned home. Father Joseph van Pelt, still remembered by some of the older members of the congregation, stayed on. He first came to Camden in the early 1950s, after ten years as a missionary in China, and finally went back to Belgium in 1995. He died the following year.

For a while, pilgrimages to Hal kept the Belgian link alive. Betty, one of the volunteers who keeps the church looking so cared for, recalls visiting the shrine at Hal and paying respects at Father van Pelt's grave. But those trips are now a thing of the past.

"As well as those of Irish origin, we have Filipinos, Africans and Poles in the congregation, and we have a service in Portuguese on Sunday evenings," says the parish priest, Father John, himself of Vietnamese heritage. "Our worshippers are from all over the world."

But there's one country of origin not now represented among parishioners, as far as Father John is aware. And that's Belgium.

8 | THE JOHNNY CASH CASH MACHINE

It's simply the best visual pun around. But even those who regularly promenade along Parkway may have missed the Johnny Cash cash machine at no. 88.

Parkway is designed for the flâneur. It boasts more boutique coffee (and tea) shops to the metre than just about any other street in the city. There are fantastic shop and pub frontages – Palmer's, the old pet (now a tea) shop, has a listed front which means the 'MONKEYS' and 'TALKING PARROTS' should have a long life; opposite, the Camden Camera Centre, now a pizza joint, is brought to mind by vintage commercial glass – a real hidden treasure, do look it out; the splendid late nineteenth century Dublin Castle is still, happily, in the beer business in its over-grand premises; but it's the unobtrusive little shop two doors down from the Castle that has caught our attention.

So here's the story behind this little gem of street art.

Camden is home to more speciality record stores – the sort that survive on love and enthusiasm (and, once upon a time, low rents) – than just about any other corner of the planet. Among them is the petite, retrobeat 'Sounds that Swing' … all-time bestseller, Stormy Gayle's 1959 number 'Flipsville', if that helps you locate the genre.

Anyway, when times were tough a few years back, the store decided to monetise its prime location on Parkway. A decent part of its frontage was given over to a cash machine.

"It said in big bold letters above the machine 'CASH'," says Neil, who runs 'Sounds that Swing'. "So we thought: what if we put the word 'Johnny' above it and a picture of Mr Cash? I cut a piece of plywood and got our very talented artist mate Ski Williams to knock up a picture of JC, and the rest is history. It's amazing how many people don't notice it though."

Ski is quite a name in music cover and poster design – specializing in extreme lettering, the sort that you might associate with West Coast concert posters of a certain vintage, and in meticulous and rather marvelous portrait drawings. He's a perfectionist, and would not wish to accept that any of his art was 'knocked up' or otherwise less than attentively executed.

"They showed me a book about Johnny Cash, and there was a page with about twenty photos of him," Ski recalls. "I love Johnny Cash – I'm a big fan. I picked one of the photos, and that's what the painting's based on."

He worked on it a day a week for six weeks or so. First drawing the Man in Black, then applying the outdoor paint with an attention grabbing dab of white to the eye, and finishing with a layer of varnish to give it all a fighting chance against the Camden Town micro-climate.

And six years later, Johnny Cash is still doling out the readies. Once you've spotted him, Johnny's sure to bring a smile to your face every time you pass by.

9 | THE MYSTERY OF THE REGENT'S PARK BARRACKS

If you walk down Albany Street from the beautiful bridge leading to Regent's Park, you will find on your left a high, forbidding yellow brick wall. It continues, uninterrupted, for a long way. Finally an arch appears, with a boom across the entrance. Above the arch is the sign: 'Regents Park Barracks'.

So what does the barracks consist of? I am afraid the Ministry of Defence has been less than forthcoming. "We would take you to any other barracks in London, but not Regent's Park," the press officer explained. Now that really whetted the appetite. There is nothing to explain what the barracks is all about beyond a pair of police in flak jackets, carrying automatic rifles, occasionally patrolling the perimeter.

Locals remember the barracks in friendlier days. Until a few years ago it was home to the Royal Horse Guards. Children were once allowed to go in and care for the horses. Troops of horses, with riders mounted at strategic intervals, would canter onto our streets for exercise in the early mornings. But the horses have gone and only the mysterious barracks remain.

So what do we know for sure? English Heritage provides this useful description of the buildings. They were constructed in 1820-21 as cavalry barracks for the Lifeguards and Artillery as part of John Nash's original design for Regent's Park.

Nash had originally intended the barracks to be situated in the northern area of the park, well away from the residential area and separated from the rest of the park by Regent's Canal. However, Nash's plan was not accepted in its entirety by the Crown with one of the changes involving a change in the location of the barracks to its present site.
Originally designed to house 450 officers and men and 400 horses the barracks were almost entirely rebuilt in 1891-93. The rebuilding followed the original general layout, and carried out under the supervision of Colonel R. Athorpe. The

layout comprises a complex of buildings arranged around a parade ground.

The only building to survive from the original barracks is the Officers' Mess which was built in 1820-21 and is situated on the east side of the parade ground. Other buildings at the northern end of the site include the Gothic chapel which was built in 1857 and the hospital which was built in 1877. Three parallel blocks used for soldiers accommodation and stables, service buildings and the riding school were all built in 1891.

Occasionally dignitaries are allowed in. In September 2013 a Conservative Member of the European Parliament was given a tour. Marina Yannakoudakis says she met members of the Royal Logistical Corps. 'The 20 Transport Squadron based at the Regent's Park Barracks provides military and road transport for the London District and includes support to the Royal Household including the Queen's Baggage Train,' she reported.

Nothing very mysterious about that: it is only when one probes a little deeper that a possible reason for the army's determination to keep prying eyes away begins to emerge. This

dates from 1980 and the most public hostage siege in modern British history.

On 30th April, six armed Iranians stormed the Iranian embassy in South Kensington. The gunmen took twenty-six people hostage and held them at gunpoint. On 5th May, in the full glare of the television cameras, elite troops of the Special Air Services (SAS) stormed the building, abseiling down from the roof. The operation lasted just seventeen minutes and all but one of the terrorists were killed.

In the aftermath of the raid the *Daily Mail* reported that the SAS soldiers were visited by the then prime minister, Margaret Thatcher. 'Returning to their temporary London quarters at Regent's Park Barracks, they were soon knocking back cans of cold beer when they were called to attention for a special visitor. Mrs Thatcher moving among them with handshakes and congratulations. "Makes us proud to be British," she told them.'

Mrs Thatcher's husband, Denis, is reported to have spoken to one of the SAS soldiers, known as 'Tom' at a later date. "He had a big grin on his face," 'Tom' explained. "You let one of the bastards live," said Denis. "We failed in that respect," Tom replied.

'Tom' was later awarded the Queen's Gallantry Medal. It was only when the medal was sold at auction by Bonhams in September 2010 that his true identity was revealed. 'Tom' was Sergeant Thomas G. C. Palmer. His medal was sold with the jacket and trousers he wore during the Iranian embassy siege, complete with SAS insignia, and a photograph of his visit to Buckingham Palace in June 1981, to receive the medal from the Queen.

Regent's Park Barracks is the London headquarters of at least one regiment of the SAS. This is what was once called the Artists Rifles, but this unit was disbanded in 1945. It became the 21 Special Air Service Regiment (Artists) (Reserve). Its responsibilities are said to include counter-revolutionary warfare and counter-terrorism, as well as close protection.

There is one final twist to this story. It is a link to Britain's first urban guerrilla group, the Angry Brigade. This unlikely movement attacked 'establishment' targets in the 1970s in protest against the Vietnam war and the conflict in Northern Ireland. On 24th September 1971 they planted a bomb outside the Regent's Park Barracks, or Albany Street Barracks as it is sometimes known.

The *International Times*, recounted their exploits. This is what the paper carried in an edition of October 1971.

> ANGRY BRIGADE LIVES!
> There was an explosion at an electricity sub-station next to the Albany Street Barracks of the Royal Corps of Transport on Friday Sept 24. According to the pigs, the sub-station was wrecked and the exterior of the barracks damaged.
> Think on that, Commander X.

The Angry Brigade seems like a voice from a very different age. Since then London has been bombed by the IRA and today faces the threat of Islamic terrorism. How much of our safety now depends on the Regent's Park Barracks? Perhaps it is best that we don't know.

10 | BLAIR'S FUNERAL

No, not that one. The other one. Eric Arthur Blair, better known as George Orwell – a socialist who surprised his friends by insisting that he should be buried 'according to the rites of the Church of England'. His funeral took place in that imposing classical-style nineteenth century church which looms rather lugubriously over Albany Street, the one with the huge doors. It's now an Orthodox cathedral.

George Orwell's connection with the Camden area dates back to 1934, when he got a job at a bookshop, Booklovers' Corner, on South End Green. The shop 'stood exactly on the

frontier between Hampstead and Camden Town', Orwell recalled, 'and we were frequented by all types from baronets to bus-conductors.' It's the model for the bookshop where Gordon Comstock works in Orwell's *Keep the Aspidistra Flying*.

Orwell initially lived above the shop, then moved to rooms in Parliament Hill and on to Lawford Road in Kentish Town – all marked by plaques – from where he made weekly visits to the public baths on Prince of Wales Road.

He moved out of the area early in 1936 – returning in the autumn of 1949, shortly after the publication of his most famous work *Nineteen Eighty-Four*, as an in-patient with his own room at University College Hospital, his lungs riddled with TB. There he spent the last few months of his life, during which he married his second wife, Sonia Brownell, while sitting up in his hospital bed and wearing a specially bought crimson corduroy jacket. He died on January 21st 1950, aged 46.

Two of his literary friends, Anthony Powell and Malcolm Muggeridge, arranged the funeral – Powell pressing his local vicar (who had apparently never heard of Orwell) to officiate. That's how the service came to be held at Christ Church in Albany Street, an 'austere classical building' in Pevsner's assessment, built in the 1830s to serve Nash's development on the east side of Regent's Park.

The funeral took place five days after Orwell's death and was by all accounts a dispiriting affair. Anthony Powell, who chose the hymns – 'All people that on earth do dwell', 'Guide me, O thou great redeemer' and 'Ten thousand times ten thousand' – recounted that for 'some reason George Orwell's funeral service was one of the most harrowing I have ever attended'. Muggeridge's account in his diary is every bit as melancholic:

> *the congregation largely Jewish and almost entirely unbelievers; Mr Rose, who conducted the service, excessively parsonical, the church unheated … a row of shabby looking relatives of George's first wife, whose grief seemed to me practically the only real element in the whole affair. The bearers who carried in the coffin seemed to me remarkably like Molo-*

> *tov's bodyguard. ... Felt a pang as the coffin was removed, particularly because of its length, somehow this circumstance, reflecting George's tallness, was poignant.*

The burial place was an Oxfordshire churchyard, where the gravestone records simply 'Eric Arthur Blair', not a hint of the name by which the occupant is much more widely known.

As for Christ Church, it fell out of use as an Anglican place of worship in 1989 and is now a cathedral in the Greek Orthodox Church of Antioch. Father Samir was ministering to a congregation of about a hundred, many of them families, at the Sunday service we attended. The liturgy was mainly in Arabic, and the worshippers were of Lebanese, Palestinian and Syrian origin. Orwell would have been intrigued!

From the inside, the church is much more pleasingly proportioned than it appears from the street. It's listed, and you can see why – with a wonderful three-sided gallery, an ornate altar piece and striking Victorian stained glass, all of which seem to be in good repair. The church is now replete with icons and candles, and services are suffused with the chanting and incense so associated with the Orthodox tradition.

There is an ease and informality about the place which was understandably absent at Orwell's funeral, a bright talent cut off at his creative zenith, and leaving a young widow and a five-year-old adopted son. It's entirely a coincidence, but how wonderfully fitting that the church, in its Orthodox guise, is now the cathedral of St George.

11 | VINOT CARS

Going back more than a century, the motor car was the preserve of the rich and motor racing even more so. And within the motoring fraternity, Vinot was about as good a model as you can find.

The company Vinot-Deguingand was established in France in 1898 as a bicycle maker, moving into the automobile business three years later. Vinot Cars was its London-based subsidiary, which used French models and English manufacturers to construct racy, pricey, but not absolutely top end, motors.

The Vinot Cars office was on Great Portland Street, London's 'Motor Row', which between the wars had more than thirty car

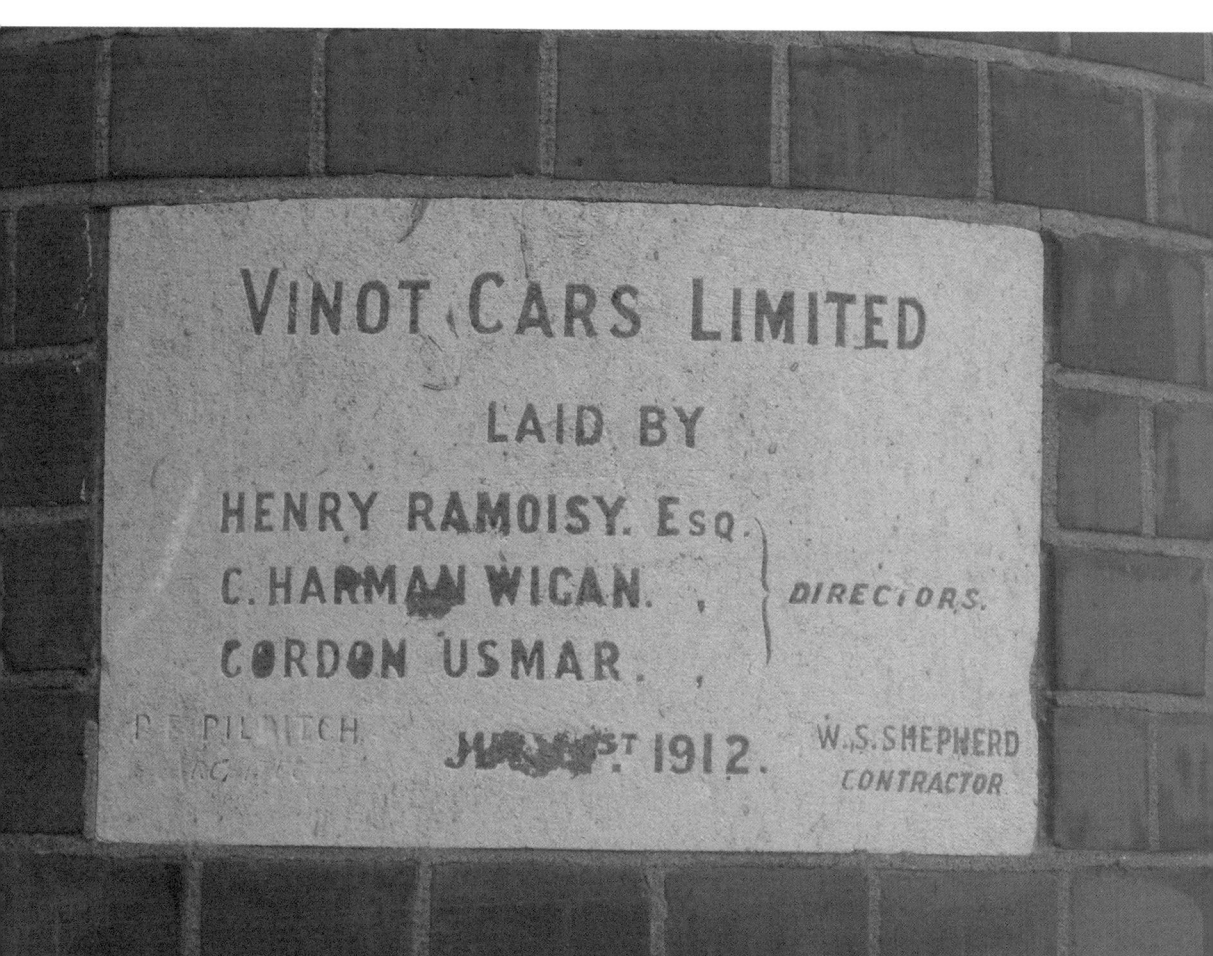

showrooms – you can see a trace of it in the design of buildings at the north end of the street, and the 'Coppen, Allen & Co' sign inlaid in the pavement. Indeed, the Retail Motor Industry Federation remains on Great Portland Street to this day.

Vinot's garage, however, was some distance away in Hammersmith – deuced inconvenient, don't you know.

Well, in 1912 Vinot Cars splashed out on a new garage and repair works in 'more central and commodious premises' just strolling distance from Great Portland Street, on Redhill Street just off Albany Street. 'These new works have been built to Messrs. Vinot's own designs', reported the *Polo Monthly*, where Vinot often took full page adverts, 'and an entirely new and up-to-date plant of machinery has been installed there.'

Certainly, this wasn't how we might now imagine a car repair works to be. The Redhill Street premises had their own foundation stone and a nifty piece of stonework above the main entrance – '19 V 12' it still reads – and were impressively and neatly constructed in red brick. How many garages still stand more than a century later?

Not that they were in use as a car repair workshop for all that long. The Vinot brand didn't last. By the early 1930s, Raleigh had taken over the site as a cycle service depot. A few years later, the buildings had been turned into a paint factory. They have now bounced back and have been spruced up as nine highly desirable flats around a courtyard which was originally a repair yard replete, one imagines, with oily rags and old tyres.

The same issue of *Polo Monthly* that reported the move to Redhill Street also gave some indication of how Vinot could afford such a well appointed garage.

> *The popularity of this well-known firm of motor manufacturers has of late years grown so rapidly, whilst the performances which both the Vinot and Gladiator cars put up in the races in which they entered last year, were so excellent that their handicap this year in all "matches" will surely be penalised at the maximum, "ten points".*

We'd certainly award the full ten points for Vinot Cars' Redhill Street repair centre – top notch in every way.

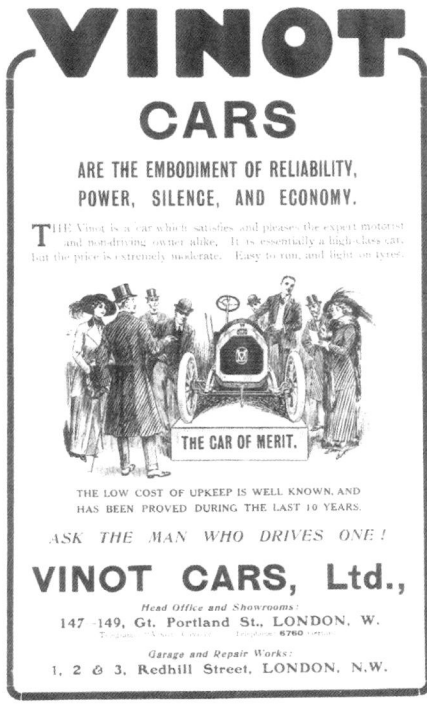

12 | MORRIS ON

It's not the sort of place you would expect the folk dance revival to take root. Not at all rustic, beyond a few stray straws of hay, nor the sort of bohemian locality which romanticises Olde England.

Morris dancing took hold in a down-at-heel corner of Camden Town simply because it was such fun. And because of a remarkable suffragist, social activist and folk dance enthusiast called Mary Neal.

She set up a girls' club, the Espérance (it means hope or expectation) Club, in Cumberland Market in the 1890s – when the hay market, established here in the 1830s and for a while the biggest in London, was still doing good business. Local girls who often laboured for a pittance in the dressmaking and tailoring trades came to 50 Cumberland Market, on the west side of the square, at the end of their working day, and of all the activities the Espérance offered, singing was what generated the most enthusiasm.

In 1905, Mary Neal called on Cecil Sharp, then new to the task of recording traditional song and now hailed as the founding figure in the folklore revival. The Espérance girls had exhausted the repertoire of Scottish and Irish song and dance – she wanted to know whether there was English folk song that they could now turn to.

Cecil Sharp had, by Mary Neal's account in her unpublished autobiography, begun collecting folk songs 'sung to him by unlettered folks in remote country villages'. One of her Espérance colleagues suggested that 'the musically unlettered members of our singing class would probably take to these songs as to no others, that they were the natural inheritance of the country folks and as there were few Londoners who were three generations away from their peasant forefathers, it might be they could learn these songs easily and with joy.'

The Somerset songs which Cecil Sharp shared with the Espérance girls were a hit, and as their Christmas concert normally involved dances, Mary Neal went back to Sharp and asked whether there were traditional dances to accompany the tunes. Yes, he said – and mentioned Morris dancers at Headington Quarry outside Oxford whom he had seen but not followed up for a more formal record.

Armed with this 'information,' Mary Neal records in her memoirs now made available digitally by the English Folk Dance and Song Society, *'I went to Oxford and arranged for two dancers to come up to London to teach their traditional Morris dances to the girls of my Club. So that the first Morris dance of that revival which has spread from one end of England to another and which is to-day part of the national life was danced at a Girl's Club in the old Cumberland Haymarket in the northwest of London. ... And that night there awoke, after generations of sleep, a little stir of an older life, an older rhythm. An older force in tune with a simpler life, a sweeter music. And that stir took place as we watched and listened to these workers of the city who sang and danced to the rhythm so long forgotten.'*

Merrie England born again – and in Camden Town!

The Espérance girls took to Morris dancing so well, and Mary Neal was such a forceful advocate, that soon they were touring and performing across the country, with boys as part of the troupe. *Punch* carried a cartoon of the girls doing a stick dance with the caption: 'Merrie England Once More'. Mary Neal published two lavish Espérance Morris books, with words, music and dance moves, along with photographs and accounts of her work and numerous favourable press notices.

There was rivalry, however, within the folk dance world. Cecil Sharp was stung by Mary Neal's penchant for publicity. He advocated a strict dance canon – she argued that dancers need to be free to interpret and adapt. And as the suffragette movement became more militant, Neal supported the campaign and described Sharp as 'violently opposed', a difference she believed made the breach between them more bitter.

When the First World War broke out in 1914, it brought an end to the Espérance dance movement. 'Our men dancers joined the army, the girls were scattered, the children could not come out in the evening because of air-raids,' Neal recalled. 'So the Club closed down and in 1918 it was impossible to begin again. The world had changed.'

For a while, 50 Cumberland Market was taken over by the Women's Freedom League and renamed the Despard Arms after the League's president, Charlotte Despard. It was described as 'a sort of model restaurant and club-rooms for men and women'. There is still a pub called the Charlotte Despard near Archway.

Mary Neal's role in the folk dance revival, for so long eclipsed by Cecil Sharp (and of course Cecil Sharp House, the splendid home of the English Folk Dance and Song Society, is on our patch), has recently become more widely acknowledged. In 1973, the women's New Espérance Morris team was formed, inspired by the legacy of Mary Neal's Espérance girls.

It dances still – but no longer at Cumberland Market.

13 | THE CUMBERLAND MARKET GROUP

Few inner London localities have disappeared as utterly as the old Cumberland Market. Not one brick survives of the buildings which surrounded the hay market a century ago. The pubs, clubs, terraced houses, Grimble's vinegar factory – all swept away many decades ago. But look harder and the trace of the market can still be seen.

The old lay-out of the area is reflected in the new development. What was the hay market is still, by-and-large, an open space, and still goes by the old name. At one end there's a community health centre, but the rest of the old market is given over to a children's play area, a fenced-in ball court and a small, simple park. Where carts would once have lined up to load with hay, the fuel of the horse-drawn transport system which kept Victorian London moving, there's now a line of outdoor personal exercise stations.

And there's more. The spot survives in the memorable paintings and drawings of artists who took the name of the Cumberland Market Group. They were neither as renowned

nor as pioneering as the Camden Town Group from which they sprang. But for Robert Bevan in particular, the most eminent of this community of artists, the market and its activity were a constant source of inspiration.

Lodgings were cheap in Cumberland Market, described by the *Daily Mirror* as 'a spot ... of mean architectural aspect', and that must have been an attraction to Bevan, who in 1914 took as a studio two rooms on the first floor at 49 Cumberland

Market, next door to the Espérance Club. But there was another incentive for an artist with a lifelong interest in horses, and who had turned to horse sales and cab stands as subject matter. There was no shortage of horses at a hay market, even one which, by this date, was past its peak.

Charlotte Mew, a poet who lived locally, wrote about the hay market in the *New Statesman* early in 1914, at just the moment Bevan was moving in to the area:

> *It is not near Piccadilly: it is a place of carts and the sky. Cabs and trains know nothing of it, and on the map you will find it very small, though it is more important than Piccadilly; it is in the real world ...*
>
> *... there is a horse-trough in the centre, cutting one of the two lines of black posts marking the road off from the great stretch of cobble-stones on either side; and one clean house with a pediment freshly painted, from which the pigeons fly. And there is the British Queen at one corner looking crossways at the King's Head at the other, and opposite the British Queen the Jolly Farmers ...*
>
> *The carts are always there: the hay-stacked carts with the empty shafts, standing like exiled ricks in a vast strange yard; and the big two- or four-horsed drays loaded with coal sacks, meal sacks, beer casks; half asleep, pulling up mechanically at the horse-trough and the Jolly Farmers*

And there it is, in Bevan's pastel shades.

Three other artists were associated with Bevan in the Cumberland Market Group: Harold Gilman, Charles Ginner and John Nash, then in his early twenties. Sixty years later, Nash reminisced about the group, and their Saturday 'at homes' in Bevan's studio:

> *It was no small honour for a young artist to be asked to join such a company of distinguished painters. At Cumberland Market, with its wide cobbled spaces and then still a staging-post for horse-drawn traffic passing across London, teas were*

dispensed every week and the four artists exhibited their work. Many artists and visitors were attracted to these gatherings and the group enjoyed considerable fame.

All sought to introduce some of the techniques of contemporary French painting to England. They exhibited as a group only once, in April 1915. Bevan gave up the Cumberland Market studio five months later, though the group – reinforced by other artists, notably C.R.W. Nevinson – continued to meet until the winter of 1918-19, when Gilman died of influenza.

Bevan's best known representation of the locality, entitled simply 'Cumberland Market, North Side', dates from 1915. It's held by the Southampton City Art Gallery, and is included here with the gallery's permission. Two other of Bevan's paintings of the market, and two drawings, are included in *A Countryman in Town: Robert Bevan and the Cumberland Market Group*, a catalogue published to accompany an exhibition at Southampton. This humble locality has been captured with more artistic skill and care than just about any other lived-in corner of the capital.

Robert Bevan died in 1925. The hay market closed a few years later. And in 1931, the buildings on the north side of the square were demolished. By the early 1950s, all the old buildings surrounding Cumberland Market had gone. But they live on in Bevan's canvases.

14 | 'DIG FOR VICTORY'

Hidden away in the middle of a Camden Town housing estate is a semi-rural idyll – 'more peaceful than Regent's Park' said one of the locals – so surprising that if you come across it by chance you have to pinch yourself to believe what you are seeing.

Hemmed in by the solid, imposing mansion blocks of the Cumberland Market estate, and on the site of what was once a canal basin, lies the largest allotment ground in central

London. Forty-six allotments in total, all actively cultivated, and dating back to the 'Dig for Victory' campaign during the Second World War.

The basin and stretch of canal leading to it were built almost 200 years ago as a spur from the Regent's Canal. Barges brought hay and straw to Cumberland Market; boats also brought in ice from Norway (there was an ice 'well' under the west side of Cumberland Market) as well as stone, timber and building materials and other supplies needed to keep the capital going. There were at one stage more than twenty wharves around the basin, as well as lots of light industry – a vinegar factory, for instance, and a ginger beer plant. Their workers lived in the terraced streets around – not the Nash terraces fronting Regent's Park, but much more modest and crowded housing to the east which has almost all been swept away.

By the 1920s, barge traffic to the basin had declined to next-to-nothing. The area took on a fly-blown demeanour. From 1928, the Crown Commissioners who owned the site began to redevelop the locality, replacing the commercial buildings with some 500 flats in seven sturdy blocks, some directly overlooking the still water-filled, but no longer commercially active, Cumberland Basin.

In the autumn of 1940, the Blitz brought devastation to the city. Much of the rubble and debris from across north London was dumped in the Cumberland Cut and Basin, which had already been drained of water and cut off from the main canal. Cumberland Market just to the south became a salvage depot, for any metal or building material that could be put to new use.

The new estate already boasted a horticultural society, for those who tended window boxes, and the Crown Commissioners had pledged that there would in time be 'large gardens, playgrounds and allotments'. The quest for plots of land to grow flowers and food has been lovingly detailed by David Hannah, one of the current cultivators (he's particularly proud of his sweet corn), in an article for the *Camden History Review*. The filling in of the canal basin was the horticultural society's opportunity. With the permission of the Crown Commissioners, though not much in the way of practical support, they levelled the basin, secured top soil (one version has it that they got 'Royal' top soil all the way from Windsor) and piped in a rudimentary supply of water.

In the course of 1941, with the organising committee sometimes resorting to air raid shelters for their meetings, the allotments began to take shape. The following spring the new tenants of the allotments decided to enter the London 'Dig for Victory' competition – the campaign to use every spare piece of land to grow food to ensure that Britain could not be starved to defeat by a sea blockade.

After the war, the allotments settled into a more stable and routine existence. In the 1950s, a handful of plots were given up to provide the site for a single storey tenants' hall – and that's still where the Cumberland Basin Horticultural Society's annual show is staged on the last Saturday in July. It's quite an event – with an overall best allotment award and lots of other categories to be competed for, from gladioli to sweet corn. Allotment holders are required to devote 60% of their plot to fruit and vegetables, perhaps an enduring echo of the 'Dig for Victory' ethos. Some four or five allotments become available on average every year, and there's quite a waiting list.

A strong community spirit shines through on these allotments, which are not hidden away on a railway siding or a scrap of marginal land but are at the heart of the estate. Everyone knows each other and enjoys a natter. On summer days, kids help out or have an impromptu picnic on their parents' plot. Patricia O'Day was preparing to grow marrows, radishes, tomatoes and sweet corn as we passed by. She's been cultivating here for twenty-five years, and is proud to have won the cup for best allotment and a host of other awards down the years.

In 2010, the Crown Estate Commissioners decided to sell Cumberland Market and three other of their London estates. Tenants were relieved when the Peabody Trust emerged as the buyer, though opinion about the new owners is now divided. The allotment holders fought hard to secure a 50-year lease on the allotments, ensuring that their valuable five acres of central London real estate will not be built on.

Having staved off one potential crisis, Cumberland Market's gardeners now face another – the spectre of HS2. The allotments themselves should survive, though with construction work round the clock just a few yards away, the striking tranquility will be gone … and the tenants' hall could be in peril.

The fighting spirit so effective in the setting-up of the allotments and in securing their future is once more in evidence to keep HS2 at bay.

15 | THE CAT GODDESSES

In a strange twist of fate, Camden's most striking architecture was the result of a discovery in the deserts of Egypt. When Howard Carter peered into a tomb in the Valley of the Kings in 1922 little did he know that he would set off a fashion for all things Egyptian. Yet the discovery of the tomb of the pharaoh Tutankhamen was to establish the most sought-after style of the day.

Standing just to the west of Mornington Crescent tube, the Black Cat factory is an outstanding example of the popularity of the style introduced by 'King Tut', as the boy pharaoh was popularly known. It was constructed for the Carreras family – Spanish refugees, who moved to London in the nineteenth century. Many Spanish liberals settled in Somers Town having fled the repressive monarchy in their own homeland. Charles Dickens (another Camden resident) refers in *Bleak House* to 'poor Spanish refugees walking about in cloaks, smoking paper cigars'.

Perhaps that is why the Carreras family went into the tobacco business. They took over a tobacconist's shop in Soho. Soon it was attracting a very exclusive clientele. King Edward VII is said to have selected his cigars at their premises at 61 Princes Street, in what is now Chinatown. The Earl of Craven was also a customer and his favourite mixture became known as 'Craven A'. It is still sold, with the brand to be found as far afield as Canada, Jamaica and North Korea.

The Carreras family prospered and by the 1920s their factory on City Road could no longer keep up with demand. Land was purchased in Camden and the architects M. E. and O. H. Collins were commissioned to build a spanking new building. The Carreras building was designed just four years after Howard Carter's sensational discoveries and the Egyptian theme proved irresistible.

The front of the building was a stylised temple, complete with Egyptian columns. It had a frieze of ten feline faces and (most striking of all) its entrance was guarded by two ten-feet-high bronze cast cats. These vast, sleek creatures were representations of the goddess Bastet – the Egyptian goddess of joy, dance, music, love ... and, of course, cats.

They were cast at the Haskins foundry in London. The immigrant family, keen to repay British hospitality, insisted that all 3,000 tons of steel used in the building was British made. The result, for all its apparent antiquity, was a modern, spacious and light building.

The factory was opened with great ceremony. The pavements in front of the building were strewn with sand to replicate the Egyptian deserts. There was a procession by members from a contemporary production of Verdi's opera Aida, with actors in ancient Egyptian costume performing around the 'temple'. There was even a chariot race on Hampstead Road.

Some 3,000 workers were employed on the site, most of them women. Raw tobacco came into the basement and was dried on the fourth floor, before being packed on the third and then despatched on the ground floor.

It was – by all accounts – a happy place to work.

"The bosses were always to be seen on the shop floor," recalls Dorothy O'Brien. "I think they really cared for the welfare of the staff." Eleanor Longhurst, who worked as a trolley-girl, agreed. "I recall being taken ill once and being taken home in the directors' chauffeur driven car." There was a dentist on the

premises, a chiropodist and a doctor – and even a convalescent home in Brighton.

Some of the workforce were part of a swimming group that went to the Prince of Wales Road baths in Kentish Town. Others were members of the Carreras Amateur Theatrical Society – putting on shows on Tottenham Court Road. The recollections of the women are housed in the Camden Local Studies and Archive Centre, having been collected by the Camden History Society as a millennium project.

Then came the war and the danger of bombing. "During World War Two," recalled William Longhurst, "enormous bomb shelters were dug out and lined with solid concrete." The shelters are still there – a vast, damp undercroft, replete with rumours that they were once linked to the underground at Mornington Crescent.

Perhaps it was all too good to last.

In 1958 the company was bought out by the Rembrandt tobacco company, a South African firm. The following year the company moved operations to a new factory at Basildon in Essex, taking one of the giant cats with them. The other was exported to Jamaica.

The staff was heartbroken at having to leave. "Many people cried," said Beatrice Rawlinson, remembering the moment when workers were informed of the relocation. But moving costs were paid and there were brand new houses to be had, and so, although many missed their London lives, they gradually became resigned to their fate.

Today the building – renamed Greater London House – has had many of its original features restored. It is now complete with replicas of the famous black cats, which once more stand proudly outside the building.

Who knows? Perhaps the goddess Bastet still stands guard over revellers enjoying themselves at Koko (once the Camden Theatre) just around the corner.

16 | RICHARD COBDEN - UNKNOWN HERO

At the scruffier, southern end of Camden High Street, amid the detritus left by the patrons of Koko, stands a forlorn figure. It is a weather-beaten, eroded statue, carved from Sicilian marble. On a granite plinth the monument stands twenty-six feet high. Anyone peering past the railing that surrounds it can read the inscription:

> Erected by public subscription to which Napoleon III was principal contributor.
> Cobden.
> Presented to the Vestry of St. Pancras, June 1868.
> Thomas Ross - Chairman of Committee
> Corn Laws repealed 1846

And, on the granite base: 'W&T Wills'.

The Cobden statue has marked the approach to Camden for almost 150 years, and nearby there's both a pub and school which also take the name of Richard Cobden (though they are probably named after the statue more than the man). Yet it is hard to find anyone who knows who he was. Sipping their early morning coffees at Costa in clear sight of this landmark, no-one had given him a second thought.

How different it was on a summer Saturday in 1868 when the statue was inaugurated.

'The site is a very fine one,' wrote the *Manchester Times* of 4th July 1868, 'and the houses in the neighbourhood were decorated with flags, giving a festive character to the proceedings. The windows and balconies of Millbrook House, the residence of Mr. Claremont, facing the statue, had been placed at the disposal of Mrs Cobden and her friends, including her three daughters.'

Three- or four-hundred subscribers who had paid for the statue to be erected had walked the short distance from the St Pancras vestry hall, in Goldington Crescent, at the bottom of Royal College Street. On their arrival they were greeted by a huge crowd, which had been entertained by the band of the North Middlesex Rifles. At half-past-three Harvey Lewis, the MP for Marylebone, stepped onto a platform covered with crimson cloth, to address the throng. There was enthusiastic cheering.

So who was the man to whom the monument was erected? And why should a French Emperor have helped pay for his statue?

Richard Cobden (1804 – 1865) was a Manchester manufacturer, with no apparent personal connection to Camden, who became a radical liberal statesman. Born into poverty, he managed to gain an education and establish himself in the cotton trade. He made a substantial fortune selling printed calico in London. But instead of increasing his wealth he embarked on travel.

With a lively intelligence he was soon deeply critical of the way in which Britain was governed. He became an advocate for free trade and peace between nations. These causes, along with education, became his passion. Cobden became a member of Parliament for Stockport in Manchester, but he is best known for three of the campaigns he waged.

The first was an attack on the corn laws, protectionist laws which forbade the import of foreign grain unless prices in the UK were sky high. Designed to maintain the wealth of landowners, the corn laws were deeply resented by townspeople. Workers resented the high price of bread and capitalists were angry that it meant having to pay higher wages. Finally, in 1846 Cobden and others managed to persuade a Conservative government to repeal the corn laws. The Anti-Corn Law League which Cobden helped to lead was one of the first mass organisations, largely of the middle class, which managed to win the day.

The second campaign was against protectionist laws between countries. Cobden worked with the French government's trade adviser Michel Chevalier. Together they skilfully persuaded the Emperor, Napoleon III, in 1860 to cut taxes on British goods in response to a reduction on the tariffs on

UNVEILING OF THE COBDEN STATUE IN HIGH-STREET, CAMDEN TOWN, ON SATURDAY LAST.—SEE

French wines. The result was a dramatic increase in trade and the French were so impressed that they subsequently signed similar treaties with a string of other countries.

Finally, Cobden was a vigorous opponent of many British military operations – whether the war against Russia in the Crimea or the notorious promotion of the opium trade with the attack on China. He was also a strong supporter of Abraham Lincoln in the American Civil War.

Despite his many achievements, Richard Cobden refused lucrative official offices, including a baronetcy and membership of the Privy Council, preferring to keep his independence.

On hearing of his death, Drouyn de Lhuys, the French minister of foreign affairs, instructed the French ambassador to express to the British government his country's 'national regret' at Cobden's demise. 'He is above all in our eyes the representative of those sentiments and those cosmopolitan principles before which national frontiers and rivalries disappear; whilst essentially of his country, he was still more of his time; he knew what mutual relations could accomplish in our day for the prosperity of peoples. Cobden, if I may be permitted to say so, was an international man.'

High French regard for this apostle of free trade explains why Napoleon III came to be the principal donor for Camden Town's foremost statue.

As we write, the statue has been removed. The area is being redeveloped and Cobden should return once the roadworks are complete, to stand once more guarding the entrance to the suburb.

17 | A BLACK REVOLUTIONARY

Walking down Eversholt Street towards Euston station, with the buses and trucks roaring past, it's a relief to turn into the quiet of Cranleigh Street. A modest, nondescript road, it boasts three blue plaques.

The first marks the early home of film director Mike Leigh (perhaps best known for 'Vera Drake' and 'Mr Turner') and actress Alison Steadman (who starred in 'Abigail's Party' and 'Gavin and Stacey'). A little further on there's a plaque commemorating the time Charles Dickens lived in a house on this site, from 1824 – 1829. As the actor Simon Callow said when he unveiled the plaque two years ago, 'Charles Dickens was really a Camden boy'. His formative years were spent here and the area was the backdrop for several of his novels.

But it is the man commemorated by the third plaque who was really fascinating. At 22 Cranleigh Street lived one of the most influential black revolutionaries of the twentieth century: George Padmore. Around his modest kitchen table, politicians and intellectuals from across Africa and the Caribbean debated and plotted. He made this flat his home from 1941 to 1957, living there with his partner, Dorothy Pizer. Both were socialists and their activities were under surveillance by the security services.

Born in Trinidad in 1903, Padmore's original name was Malcolm Ivan Meredith Nurse. He took his pseudonym while at university in Washington, when he became active in the American Communist Party. This was the beginning of his revolutionary career. Now known as Padmore, he was soon a rising star in the movement. In 1929 he was sent to Moscow, becoming head of the 'Negro Bureau' of the Red International of Labour Unions. Padmore was elected a member of the Moscow City Soviet, before moving to the German port of Hamburg to edit a monthly, *The Negro Worker*.

Germany in the 1930s was no easy place for a black revolutionary. His offices were ransacked and he was deported to Britain. It was around this time that his fervour for Soviet Marxism faded. Disillusioned with Moscow's failure to promote the cause of colonial peoples, Padmore left the movement – wisely refusing an invitation to explain himself before a disciplinary panel of the Comintern, which would almost certainly have seen him executed.

Still fiercely critical of colonialism, Padmore took up residence in France and then Britain. Padmore's first London home was in Vauxhall Bridge Road before moving to Guilford Street, near Russell Square and then making his home in Cranleigh Street during the Second World War. He wrote *How Britain Rules Africa* – one of his many books and pamphlets attacking imperialism. With his friend and fellow Trinidadian author, C.L.R. James, Padmore founded the International African Friends of Ethiopia following Italy's invasion of the country in 1935.

These were hard times for Padmore, who eked out a living by giving classes for colonial students who paid small sums for the privilege. He made contact with the left of the British Labour Party. The radical MP Fenner Brockway, who led the Movement for Colonial Freedom, was one of his many friends and supporters. Although keeping up a blistering attack on British foreign policy, Padmore was a welcome guest at Labour Party summer schools.

Perhaps unsurprisingly, given his past, British intelligence kept a file on Padmore. They issued bulletins to the colonies about what he was up to and kept a close watch on his activities. One meeting was addressed both by the famous African-American pan-Africanist, W.E.B. du Bois and the future president of Kenya, Jomo Kenyatta – 'all well-known negro extremists', according to the note on Padmore's file. Some of the information was less than accurate, including warnings about a non-existent 'Pan-African Brotherhood' that Padmore was supposed to have formed.

Padmore's closest links were with his African and Caribbean friends, including the future president of Ghana, Kwame Nkrumah, then studying in London. 'We used to sit in his small kitchen,' Nkrumah later recalled, 'the wooden table completely covered by papers, a pot of tea which we always forgot until it had been made two or three hours, and George typing at his small typewriter so fast that the papers were churned out as though they were rolled off a printing press.'

The hall was decorated with the following slogans:-

"Oppressed peoples of the earth - unite".
"Freedom of all subject peoples".
"Africa speaks".
"Africa, arise".
"African peoples - Four freedoms".
"Down with Imperialism".
"Down with Trusteeship".
"Down with colour bar".
"Down with lynching".
"Ethiopia wants exit to the sea".
"Freedom of the Press in the Colonies".

Dr. W.E.B. Du BOIS, leader of the American Negro Association, presided over the conference, and among the speakers were PADMORE, ABRAHAM, Wallace JOHNSON, Jomo KENYATTA (all well-known negro extremists) Chief A.S. COKER, Magnus WILLIAMS and Amigha WASHUKU (Nigerian trade unionists), Mrs. RENNER (a barrister from Lagos), J.E. APPIAH (West African Students Union), Ashie NIKOI (Gold Coast), Garba JUHUMPA (Gambia), Malm LUBI (a Zulu), Alma LABADIE (Jamaica), F.J. Du PLAU (a

In 1947 Nkrumah returned to Ghana (then known as Gold Coast) and soon came to lead the independence movement. Padmore continued their relationship, writing him long letters of advice. When Ghana reached independence in 1957, Padmore went to live in Accra as a presidential adviser. But it was not an entirely happy experience. Ghanaians resented his influence and he was less than pleased with the salary he was offered. Nonetheless his relationship with Nkrumah held firm.

In 1959 Padmore was found to be suffering from cirrhosis of the liver and was flown back to London for treatment, but the disease was terminal and in September he died. On learning of his death Nkrumah went on Ghana radio. 'One day, the whole of Africa will surely be free and united,' he told his listeners, 'and when the final tale is told, the significance of George Padmore's work will be revealed.' Nkrumah paid to have the kitchen table on which they had shared so much to be shipped from Cranleigh Street to Accra.

The blue plaque in Cranleigh Street was unveiled in June 2011 at a ceremony attended by the high commissions of Trinidad and Tobago and Ghana. Selma James, widow of his old friend C.L.R. James, told the crowd: 'Every anti-colonial activist organising against British imperialism came to 22 Cranleigh Street.'

18 | WORKING MEN'S COLLEGE - FADING AWAY

The proud legacy of the best that Christian socialism could offer the world of further education stands at the junction of Camden Street and Crowndale Road. The Working Men's College claims the title of Europe's oldest functioning adult education establishment. It has an illustrious pedigree, having been founded in 1854. Its Victorian benefactors had the laudable aim of bringing education to the working poor.

But the college's current governors appear a little uneasy about its heritage. Its title has been changed to: 'WMC – The Camden College'. There is an apparent desire to sweep its past under the carpet and rebrand it as a twenty-first century institution.

Its original inspiration came from the Labour and Co-operative movement. The aim was to provide the working class with a liberal education. The first classes included algebra and geometry, the structure and functioning of the human body,

Latin, English and law. Its twin, the Working Women's College (founded in 1874), was absorbed into the older institution in 1967. This was only two years after the Working Men's College allowed its first female students to join its classes.

The Working Men's College's early supporters were certainly illustrious. They included the artist Dante Gabriel Rossetti, the political economist John Stuart Mill, and Charles Kingsley, author of *The Water-Babies*. John Ruskin was 'the distinguished and superior director' of the drawing class. It was he who encouraged his pupils 'to note and observe, to perceive, and not merely to see, the wonder and beauty of this mysterious universe into which we are born.' William Morris came to speak on socialism. George Orwell gave lectures during the Second World War. Seamus Heaney, the poet, was among its volunteers.

The original address was 31 Red Lion Square in Holborn. The college moved to Great Ormond Street in 1857 but it

needed purpose-built premises and in 1904 the distinguished architect William Douglas Caroe came up with this fine design. The institution's title, Working Men's College, was proudly incorporated into its façade.

Today the original entrance has been abandoned. The new entrance and reception area is far larger and lighter, but hardly sympathetic to the rest of the building. The foundation stone, laid by the Prince of Wales, is to be found next to the dustbins. The impressive library contains bookcases salvaged from Great Ormond Street. But it is filled with volumes on the ascent of Everest and biographies of imperial heroes – like General Smuts – that are hardly, if ever, consulted.

Perhaps the changes the college is undergoing are an attempt to reflect the changing nature of Camden's 'working poor'. The college now sees its purpose as serving the area's diverse communities. Courses in hairdressing and beauty therapy have replaced Greek and Latin. Newcomers can improve their English and computing skills. Around 3,000 students use the college and its work has been highly rated by Ofsted. But its hall contains faint echoes of a different past. The names of the recipients of past prizes and medals are carved into the wood panelling – a tradition that has long since been abandoned.

The Working Men's College gives the impression of being faintly disdainful of its illustrious past; focusing instead on a more functional, but less high-minded and ambitious, future.

19 | THE SHADOW OF A SHADOW

Walking away from St Pancras and King's Cross along Crowndale Road towards the bright lights of Camden there stands on the right the familiar white building of Theatro Technis. Once part of the Anglican church estate, it has been the home to the Cypriot theatre company since 1978. But before you go in to watch one of its productions, have a look at its side wall. There – if you look hard – you will see traces of what was once a giant mural.

Today only the barest outlines can be discerned. This is the faded remnant of a huge work of protest that was etched onto the side of the building in 1987. It was the handiwork of Paul Donnelly and Geoff Staden and was London's answer to a movement that began in the United States.

"They came to see me," recalls George Eugeniou, with a smile. He has been the artistic director and driving force behind Theatro Technis since he founded the theatre group in a garage in 1957. Paul and Geoff explained that they wanted to join the movement to commemorate the victims of the bombing of

Hiroshima, but needed a large wall to work on. "They wanted to use the side of the building, so I said 'yes, you are welcome – go ahead.'"

The mural was the two artists' contribution to the International Shadow Protest Movement which was inspired by the images of people vaporised by the nuclear explosion at Hiroshima on 6th August, 1945. Blackened shadows were all that remained of those victims of the blast who were within 300 metres of ground zero and experienced the most searing heat.

The Shadow Project began in Portland, Oregon in 1982 and was taken up across the world three years later. Artists found various ways of placing memorials in 426 cities around the world, and this was one that found a home in Camden.

The Peace Pledge Union (which has been campaigning against all wars since 1934) has a website which includes what appears to be the only photograph of the mural in its original form. It shows the painting stretching almost to the roof of the front building and comes with this helpful explanation:

The figures at Theatro Technis are sandblasted onto the wall. 'Peace' is written in English, Greek, Turkish, Irish, Chinese and Bengali - the principal languages spoken in the area. For people at the Theatro Technis a peace mural has more of an immediate significance than the threat of nuclear war. Since the coup in 1979 Cyprus has been divided into two hostile camps. One day we hope to see a united and peaceful Cyprus restored.

As the years have gone by and Camden's rain and grime have taken their toll the images have faded. Today all that remains of Paul and Geoff's work is a plaque and the faintest of human outlines – particularly the hands commemorating the victims of Hiroshima. The atomic bomb killed at least 66,000 people in Hiroshima and more than 30,000 at Nagasaki; some estimates put the numbers far higher. No-one is certain as the population records were reduced to dust.

20 | A MOVEMENT THAT SHOOK THE WORLD

Painted on the door of a building on a Camden side street is a familiar image: a smiling, confident Nelson Mandela, fist held aloft. Above him a quote: 'It always seems impossible until it's done.'

The mural is, appropriately enough, at 13 Mandela Street, home to the Anti-Apartheid Movement for the last decade of its existence. This piece of street art is almost all there is to see of the organisation, which was based in the borough of Camden for all its 35-year history. Camden was – as one journalist put it – the 'battleground borough' when it came to fighting apartheid. Many in the movement lived in the area and Camden politicians were in the forefront of its campaigns down all those long years.

Nelson Mandela himself came in 2003 and unveiled a blue plague at 13 Lyme Street (not far away) commemorating Joe Slovo and Ruth First, two leading members of the South African Communist Party and African National Congress. President Mandela, as he then was, remembered Joe as 'level-headed, a courageous comrade – he was a hero'. He recalled Ruth as a 'sharp lady' who didn't suffer fools gladly. He bore the 'scars' of her criticism, he told the crowd, which included the Holborn and St Pancras MP, Frank Dobson.

It was no accident that Anti-Apartheid was formed in Camden. In 1950 the Communist Party of South Africa was declared illegal by the newly-elected apartheid government. The communists decided to dissolve the party and many went into exile. A good number established new lives in this part of London. It was to take three years before those comrades who stayed behind re-formed the party as an underground organisation, subtly changing the name to the South African Communist Party.

The communists living in the safety of London felt they should do what they could. On 26th June 1959 the exiles, together with British supporters, met in Holborn Hall on the corner of Gray's Inn Road and Theobalds Road. They decided to launch a boycott of South African goods and were given an office in a basement at 200 Gower Street. This was the surgery of a GP from Grenada, Dr David Pitt.

The boycott movement was launched in March 1960. It won the support of the Labour and Liberal parties and the Trades Union Congress. But it was events in South Africa that were to really transform the campaign into a fully-fledged movement. On 21st March 1960 police opened fire on a protest at Sharpeville, leaving sixty-nine people dead.

A wave of revulsion swept around the world and hundreds protested outside the South African embassy, on Trafalgar Square. The following month Anti-Apartheid was officially born. The Labour MP Barbara Castle became the first presi-

dent. An arson attack at the Gower Street premises (the first of several organised by the South African authorities) led the movement to seek new premises – this time with the National Union of Students, at 15 Endsleigh Street.

In 1964 the movement – which had grown considerably – moved again: this time to 89 Charlotte Street, behind Goodge Street tube station. Ronnie Kasrils (later a minister in Mandela's government) plotted the downfall of the apartheid government in pubs around the area, while at the same time perfecting small explosions for leaflet bombs on Hampstead Heath.

It was in January 1983 that Anti-Apartheid moved to its final home in Mandela Street. At the time the address was Selous Street, which had particularly unfortunate connotations, since the Selous Scouts were an elite unit in the Rhodesian army. In fact the street was named after the Camden Town artist of the Victorian era, Henry Courtney Selous, but it was clearly an embarrassment. So – led by Camden councillor Hugh Bayley – a campaign was launched which finally resulted in the street being re-named.

The one constant throughout most of Anti-Apartheid's history was the slightly dishevelled figure of Mike Terry. A former leader of the National Union of Students, he served as executive secretary from 1975 until the movement was finally wound up in October 1994. Always to be found struggling with a mountain of papers, he was the driving force behind a movement that can truly claim to have changed British public opinion and mobilised the world.

The successor to Anti-Apartheid, the Action for Solidarity with South Africa has, sadly, abandoned Camden for Islington. Perhaps it is some consolation that it is run by a former leader of Camden council, Tony Dykes.

21 | THE FINAL CHORD

What was Camden once famous for? Not just markets, and rail lines – it once housed the main manufacturers of cheap, upright pianos. From the mid-nineteenth century, just about every aspiring middle-class household had a piano in the parlour. It was as much a symbol of gentility as the aspidistra. And many were made here in Camden, where the rail and canal links were perfect for transporting such bulky items. There are still any number of former piano works around.

But the rise of the gramophone, and then TV, pushed the old 'joanna' out of most middle-class homes. Polish- and East German-made pianos, and later imports from China and South Korea, undercut the domestic industry, and electric keyboards, both cheaper and more mobile, also ate into the demand for the old fashioned acoustic kind.

Between the wars, the Mother Redcap pub (now the World's End) was reputed to be an informal labour exchange for piano workers. If you were on the look-out for a job, that was the place to go. Even then, the industry was on a downward slope.

Heckscher & Company, a supplier to the piano industry, was Camden's last toehold in the trade. Martin Heckscher recalls that his father was advised in the early 1930s that 'there was no future in the piano industry'. But the Heckschers were born into pianos. Siegmund Heckscher, a migrant from Hamburg, set up the company in 1883, and it moved to Bayham Street early in the last century. In the early 1970s, Martin himself joined the family business, supplying specialist piano parts.

"The '70s and '80s were pretty good decades for us," he recalls, "because piano restoration was thriving and the surviving factories were still in production. I think we were a workforce of about eight by 1989. However it was all gradually downhill from that point onwards."

Downhill to the point that in July 2014, Heckschers left its longstanding Bayham Street home – Camden's last link with what was once its staple industry had been broken.

"There is no escape from commercial reality," Martin Heckscher reflects. "The piano industry had diminished year on year, and we had traded at a loss for some time. It was impossible to generate enough profit to cover the costs of keeping the doors open. I look back and realise that if we had been a hardnosed 'proper' business we would have closed the doors between five and ten years earlier, but we were a close knit little team and making the decision to cease trading was extremely difficult."

Martin now runs a slimmed down, one-man operation from home.

As we write, the Heckscher & Company signage is still on display at 75 Bayham Street – a last vestigial emblem of the piano trade. But by the time you read this, that final chord may well have faded away.

22 | ST MARTIN'S ALMSHOUSES

When St Martin-in-the-Fields, the imposing church near Trafalgar Square, ran out of space to bury its dead, it turned to the pastures of Camden Town. In 1805, two fields known as Upper Meadow and Upper Brook Meadow on the north side of what's now Pratt Street were consecrated as an additional burial ground for the central London parish. It became known as the Camden Town Cemetery. It's now the tranquil, well-maintained St Martin's Gardens.

Having got a toehold in north London, St Martin-in-the-Fields decided to make the most of it. The western-most slice of the burial plot, still free of interments, was built on from 1817 to provide new almshouses for the deserving poor among the parish's elderly women. That satisfyingly symmetrical terrace of nine almshouses, each originally with eight rooms, is one of the architectural gems of our area – a little hidden away on Bayham Street behind a substantial hedge and a locked gate, but worth an admiring gaze.

Initially more than seventy women were crammed in to the almshouses – though from mid-century, the residents were allowed a little more living room, and in about 1880 a chapel, small infirmary and matron's residence were added as a second row of buildings, even more hidden away from prying eyes.

The regime was strict: all residents were required to maintain their standing as 'persons of good character', which no doubt explains the requirement that 'no almswoman may expose anything out of her window (pots of flowers excepted)'. And the matron locked all the residents in, and everyone else out, overnight.

In mid-century, St Martin-in-the Fields made further attempts to develop sections of the meadow not already used for burials (interments stopped in the 1850s). St Martin's Tavern on Pratt Street – the signage is still prominent on the building though it closed as a pub in the 1980s and is now a Japanese restaurant – was one such intrusion on the cemetery grounds, which is why it was nicknamed 'The Bone House'.

In another corner of the meadow, builders disturbed – and desecrated, by all accounts – dozens of recent burials so greatly annoying local residents that they threw stones at the labourers and angrily insisted, successfully, that the work stop.

In 1889, the graveyard was laid out as a garden – opened by the Countess of Rosebery, a Rothschild by birth and reputed to be the richest woman in England whose husband became a Liberal prime minister. A new memorial was erected to the dramatist and song-writer Charles Dibdin, who is buried here, and several other of the more imposing graves and memorials were retained. The gardens were spruced up by Camden council a few years back, and in a nice nod to the past in 2006 the current Countess of Rosebery, the granddaughter-in-law of Hannah Rothschild, presided over the re-dedication of the area as a public garden.

As for the almshouses, they pottered on – though the property was not always well maintained, and the full complement of deserving elderly women were not always in residence. In 1980, the charity which ran the almshouses decanted the matron and remaining residents to St John's Wood – where it continues to provide accommodation much as originally intended, though now for men as well. By then squatters – who had already taken over several houses in the area – had moved in to the empty properties. They apparently got on well with the last of the almswomen who were, we're told, 'very good humoured and enjoyed a gossip'.

Eventually the properties were sold – though the new owners had quite a task in making the houses habitable. "The last squatters were a tribe of glue sniffers who finally set the place on fire, which is how I was able to afford to buy it," recounts one resident who has clocked-up thirty-five years at the almshouses. "An upstairs window was missing courtesy of the fire brigade, the ground floor was flooded courtesy of lead thieves cutting the water main, and there were dozens of plastic bags full of Evo-Stik. I met the last of the women residents and the matron while I was working on the house but they had moved on before I actually moved in."

The little chapel – you can see it from St Martin's Gardens – was in a particularly bad state, and at one point was apparently listed as a dangerous structure. It has been wonderfully restored and extended as a home, complete with the original paved floor, saracenic style windows and carved pulpit. St Martin's chapel is – to our eyes – ever bit as nice as that grand edifice from which it got its name.

23 | THE EOKA PRIEST

A priest flown out of Britain at the dead of night for political reasons. Questions asked in parliament – newspaper journalists on the chase – church leaders concerned – Camden's Cypriot community deeply hurt.

This was the summer of 1956, when EOKA guerillas were fighting to end British rule in Cyprus and for the island's union with Greece. The clergyman at the heart of the row was Kallinikos Macheriotis, the archimandrite (literally – the head of a flock of sheep, actually – senior priest) at the Greek Orthodox church of All Saints, the beautiful neo-Grecian (how appropriate!) church which stands at the junction of Camden Street and Pratt Street.

The church has a stand-out tower and a real elegance, especially if seen from a distance – from St Martin's Gardens, say – and is one of the few Grade 1 listed buildings on our patch. Constructed in the early 1820s, the church was known initially as Camden Chapel. It became an Orthodox place of worship in 1948 and is now the Greek Orthodox cathedral church of All Saints.

Cypriot migration to London increased sharply after the Second World War. Greek Cypriots tended to congregate in Camden, Turkish Cypriots in Stoke Newington and on Green Lanes. The political turbulence on the island prompted more Cypriots to leave, and the concern among Cypriot ex-pats about what was happening back home was intense.

The church was the focus of the community and Father Macheriotis was described as the unofficial leader of London's Greek Cypriots. So it was a big deal when he was deported from the country 'in the public interest' on a flight to Athens leaving at 1:45 in the morning.

The government didn't immediately give any reason for the late-night move beyond saying that the priest's activities had gone far beyond any legitimate ecclesiastical duties. A Greek diplomat protested against the exclusion, and the Greek Orthodox church in London expressed consternation: 'We are

shocked, and cannot understand why he was deported. He was apparently given no notice.'

Alongside the report on the deportation in *The Times* was a much briefer news report of the death of three British soldiers in a mine explosion near Limassol. In total, more than a hundred British servicemen died during the four years of EOKA violence, along with police, civilians and members of the armed group.

The Conservative home secretary of the day was eventually obliged, by the political fire storm which erupted, to give reasons for the deportation. He said that Father Macheriotis headed a committee which collected funds in England 'for the Cyprus national struggle', that his church in Camden Town had become 'a centre for the dissemination of anti-British propaganda', and unwelcome pressure had been brought to bear on 'loyal Cypriot and Greek nationals living in London'.

The Cyprus-born priest, for his part, gave a news conference in Greece where he insisted that the fund was for 'Cypriot families in distress' and that donations were absolutely voluntary and quite legitimate.

One angry Labour MP who had taken a keen interest in the Cyprus issue declared: 'My own information is that not one penny of the money he collected has left this country, that he had no connection whatever with EOKA and that his so-called "anti-British activities" were no more than an expression of sentiments shared by the great majority of his Greek compatriots.'

All Saints remained the focus of the Greek Cypriot community in Camden Town and beyond. In 1960, Cyprus became independent with a leading clerical figure, Archbishop Makarios, as its first president. He often preached at All Saints when visiting London, and on his death in August 1977, an estimated 6,000 mourners attended a service there, most standing outside in the rain. Hundreds of Cypriot-run shops, restaurants and businesses across Camden closed for the day of the funeral.

And Father Macheriotis? Well, he was given a parish in Athens and then was recalled to Cyprus as a bishop. In 1968

– so *The Times* reports – he returned to London as a representative of the Cypriot church at the Lambeth Conference. "I think I was a political scapegoat," he declared looking back on the events of June 1956. "Anyway I have no ill feelings. I was only sad that I had to leave my people in such a hurry."

The authorities here had no ill feelings either, it seems, for the bishop was invited to a Buckingham Palace garden party during his stay.

24 | LAWFORD'S WHARVES

The 200-year-old Regent's Canal was once the main commercial artery weaving through Camden – with lots of wharves, industry and homes too. Once again in recent years, after decades of neglect, the canal has been seen as an asset and fashionable new flats have been built on its banks. But precious few of the old canal-side houses have survived. If you want to see the very best of what's left then make your way to Lyme Terrace, just south of Camden Road, where there's a row of five impressive early Victorian houses high above the canal, and from that footpath look across the water to Lawford's Wharf.

It wasn't a wharf, it was two wharves – the College and Devonshire wharves – and the ghost sign still visible from Lyme Street reads 'Lawford & Sons Wharves'. John Eeles Lawford (don't ask where that bizarre middle name came from) set up as a slate merchant on Euston Road in 1840. He seems to have got involved in speculative building in and around Camden. By 1860, the family firm was established by the canal where it remained for well over a century. A 1914 commercial directory lists Lawford & Sons as 'lime, cement and general building material merchants'.

When the wharves were redeveloped a decade or more back on a site then described as a derelict builders' yard, two rather startling curved blocks, mixed offices and flats, were built in distinctly nautical style, with prows, portholes and all manner of maritime references. It might have been wonderful at Tilbury or Wapping but doesn't immediately make sense along a canal. Nevertheless, it managed to get a design award – and it's certainly better than your average north London new build.

After a bit of a battle, the developers were obliged to retain two splendid workers' cottages, probably from the first half of the nineteenth century and deservedly listed by English Heritage. There they are still – facing the canal, when both Lyme Street and Royal College Street ostentatiously face away, and their pastel shade of aquamarine punctuating the profile of those two bulkier and much more recent additions to the wharf site.

Lawford's Wharf is now a top-end, gated development, and on the occasion we managed to get ourselves shown round, access was further restricted by an aggressive goose whose partner was incubating on a nearby nest. The cottages would make wonderful homes, but Camden council won't wear that – so both buildings are offices, one for a shoe design company and the other taken by lawyers. The buildings (there's a suggestion that one, perhaps both, were once lock keepers' cottages – but that may be developers' licence) are double-fronted and distinctly more imposing than your average cottage, but are surprisingly shallow, just one small room deep, and with a curious clerical-style pointed window on the rear wall.

"It's a great location," says one of those working in what are now known as Lawford's Wharf Cottages – while going on to mention the time a body was pulled out of the water close by, and the brothel down the way which recently closed down.

The greatest thing about these canal cottages is that they have survived.

25 | THE CAMDEN TOWN MURDER

There's nothing the popular press likes more than a good murder mystery – and the killing of Emily Dimmock in her bed, naked, her throat cut from ear to ear, fitted that bill in every regard. Emily (also known as Phyllis) was a 22-year-old blonde-haired woman who worked occasionally as a prostitute. She lived, and died, at 29 St Paul's Road, since renamed Agar Grove – a house which on the exterior remains much as it did when the murder created a sensation in September 1907.

Emily's common-law husband discovered the body on return from a night shift. On the table lay the remains of a meal shared by two people. Emily had spent the evening at a pub, the Eagle on Royal College Street – it's still there – then returned home, had sex, and was killed while sleeping. The basin on the washstand had been used to rinse out the blood on the victim's petticoat, which the killer had apparently used to clean his hands.

The papers immediately christened this the 'Camden Town Murder' – even *The Times* adopted that sensational shorthand. The case had sex, gore and an apparently motiveless crime. And it bore the echo of the Jack the Ripper murders in the East End nineteen years earlier.

Better still for the police papers, and in those days there were publications with titles such as the *Illustrated Police News*, there was a courtroom drama too. Robert Wood, a commercial designer, was put on trial for murder at the Old Bailey. He had certainly met Emily during the evening at the Eagle, and it was not their first such encounter. Some of the strongest evidence against him came from his girlfriend who described herself, perhaps euphemistically, as an artist's model. There was little direct evidence to link him to the murder – but the exposure of his false alibi didn't help him.

The case caught the popular imagination. The public gallery was filled to capacity throughout. One paper spoke breathlessly of 'the most remarkable criminal trial held within the past fifty years'. Wood's barrister, Sir Edward Marshall Hall, delivered a powerful defence, taking advantage of new legislation which allowed the defendant to take to the stand to give evidence on his own behalf. It made his court room reputation and saved his client's life.

The judge in his summing up initially appeared to be pointing towards conviction:

> *The woman must have been murdered by a man who was leading a double life. ... the whole of the evidence seemed to him to point to the fact that the prisoner had been leading a double life, for although he had been highly spoken of as a man of excellent reputation, yet he now seemed to have been in the habit of frequenting a place where harlots resorted*

But he went on to insist that the only evidence against Wood was circumstantial and allowed for 'reasonable doubt' and he more-or-less ordered the jury to acquit. After retiring for just fifteen minutes, that's what they did.

Living about a mile away from the scene of the murder was the renowned artist Walter Sickert. In his rooms at Mornington Crescent, he often painted a model nude on the bed. As the art historian Lisa Tickner has demonstrated, Sickert was also fascinated by detective mysteries and unsolved crime, and had a particular interest in the Jack the Ripper case after his landlady told him she was convinced that a previous tenant had been the serial killer.

Sickert painted several oils based on, and some taking their title from, the Camden Town Murder. They depict a clothed man with the naked body of a woman on a bed. There was no

overt violence, more a documentary-style representation of the aftermath of a sad and sordid death in a squalid ill-lit room.

The artist knew no more about what happened at 29 St Paul's Road than he had read in press reports and seen in the lurid, and themselves simply impressionistic, illustrations in the police papers. He was a prominent member of the Camden Town Group of artists and some of these canvasses were displayed in their debut exhibition in 1911 – prompting a censure from the *Daily Telegraph* that his 'choice of subjects [was] more worthy of the "Police News" than a picture gallery of high rank'. Sickert delivered a riposte in a lecture many years later:

> It is said that we are a great literary nation but we really don't care about literature, we like films and we like a good murder. … Not that I am against that because I once painted a whole series about the Camden Town murder, and after all murder is as good a subject as any other.

As for the more recent suggestion that Sickert's paintings were a silent confession of his involvement in the Jack the Ripper murders, well, that hasn't won much favour among Ripperologists.

26 | THE ETERNAL OPTIMISTS

Dum pli ol duonjarcento, Camden estas la centro de la Esperanto-Movado en Londono.

Let me say that again – in English this time: For well over half-a-century, Camden has been the hub of the Esperanto movement in London.

Esperanto is the universal language devised by a Polish ophthalmologist, L.L. Zamenhof, in the 1880s. It was born out of

his anguish about the division language caused in his home town:

> In Białystok the inhabitants were divided into four distinct elements: Russians, Poles, Germans and Jews (he wrote); each of these spoke their own language and looked on all the others as enemies. In such a town a sensitive nature feels more acutely than elsewhere the misery caused by language division and sees at every step that the diversity of languages is the first, or at least the most influential, basis for the separation of the human family into groups of enemies

Ever since the first Esperanto grammar was published in 1887, it's been associated with an ideal of fraternity and friendship across barriers of language and nation. A way of bringing the world together.

The London Esperanto Club got going in 1903, and it's still going – though for a movement which aspires to be universal, it's always been a little, well, niche. Club membership peaked in the early 1930s at about 330. It now stands at just over fifty. And on the Friday I popped round the attendance was just five.

But as one of the group put it to me, 'esperanto' means optimist.

From 1936, the Esperanto Club met on Drummond Street near Euston, sharing the premises of another idealist organization, the Cooperative (later Countrywide) Holidays Association. "We were happy there," says Terry, active in the Esperanto movement for more than half-a-century. But in October 2004, not long after celebrating the Club's centenary, Esperantists were forced out of their home when the building was demolished to make way for flats.

For the past decade, the London Esperanto Club has been meeting at the Irish Centre on leafy Camden Square – itself a Camden institution stretching back sixty years. Terry and his Slovenian wife Anica make the journey in most Fridays from Milton Keynes. Esperanto was what brought them together – they met at an international congress in 1964, and it was then the only language they shared. They brought their children up to speak Esperanto. When they celebrated their silver wedding at the club, there were twenty other couples present who had met through Esperanto. It really is a family affair.

And a movement of the left? Yes, very broadly, say Club members – though one recalls that in his early days, followers of the right-wing libertarian Ayn Rand then rallied to the Esperanto standard. "I'm motivated by a sense of fairness," Terry insists – "it's not fair to expect everyone to speak English".

At the Irish Centre, Esperantists take it in turns to talk about their enthusiasms or areas of expertise – so there have been lectures on such wide-ranging topics as East Timor, the music of Scott Joplin and the hacking movement. The night we dropped in was a games evening – a card game with dice, one of the cards showing a giant jellyfish (*gigantaj meduzoj* in Esperanto), which took quite a bit of explaining, and since the whole point was to encourage conversation in Esperanto, it fulfilled its purpose.

27 | SHERLOCK'S TEMPLE

Tucked away on the north side of Rochester Square is a small church, now sadly padlocked and deserted, built with the help of Sherlock Holmes. A spiritualist temple, no less – in danger of going over to the other side.

Sir Arthur Conan Doyle, the creator of Sherlock Holmes, was one of the most high profile spiritualists in the period after the First World War, when the huge number of casualties prompted many thousands to try to make contact with those they had loved and lost. One of Conan Doyle's sons died in 1918 of pneumonia two years after being badly wounded on the Somme.

In the early 1920s, according to the Spiritualists' National Union which proclaims itself the country's fifth biggest non-conformist church (a perplexing claim, who's counting?), Conan Doyle used some £400 of his considerable wealth – in part from the global success of his Sherlock Holmes stories – to buy a plot of land in Camden as the site of a spiritualist church. He doesn't seem to have had a personal connection with the area beyond being a benefactor.

The local spiritualist movement raised a still bigger amount to build the temple, a small, unostentatious building with a large lunette window. And Conan Doyle came along on October 30th 1926 to lay the foundation stone. Another stone was laid by a newspaper editor and celebrity theatre critic, Hannen Swaffer.

In case you are not entirely clear what spiritualism is, here's what the SNU says: 'to some it is a philosophy, to some a religion, to some the science behind mediumship and evidence of life after death ... to some it is the life long study and attainment of spiritual wisdom'. So now we've got that sorted ...

In its heyday, the Rochester Square temple had a congregation of well over a hundred. But that's a long time back. When *The Times* columnist Alan Coren ventured by in 1989, he found himself alongside twenty elderly ladies for an afternoon of clairvoyance presided over by a medium,

Mrs Denny, 'a trim and cheerful lady in a brown twin-set':

> *A number of husbands came through, occasionally identified by name, and in one case by the size of his head (small), and then Mrs Denny looked at me. ...*
> *But nobody came. All that Mrs Denny said was: "Don't worry about your financial problems, your spirit friends tell me they will help."*
> *A number of heads turned to gaze at me, sympathetically. I wondered if I looked like a man whose money had just died.*

More recently, the dwindling congregation was further troubled by a bit of a bust-up. "All perfectly normal for spiritualists," insists our contact at head office. "If you haven't fallen out with everybody, you're not it."

The last spiritualist service in the temple was in 2013, and since then the building's been locked up – though with a spir-

itualist library apparently bequeathed by Conan Doyle still in situ. For a few weeks, some new age squatters, the Rainbow Family of Living Light, took up residence, but they were eventually prised out.

The Spiritualists' Union is talking of getting planning permission for a three bedroom house in the back garden, and says it will use the proceeds to renovate the temple and make it available for community use as well as worship.

That really would be life after death.

28 | ÉCOLE DE POLE

'École de Pole' it said discreetly on an otherwise anonymous door along one of those mews-style back streets where Kentish Town edges into Camden. Curious place for a Polish language school, we thought. Even stranger that it announces its purpose in a third language.

Then the penny dropped. Aided by closer inspection of the school logo.

"That's me in heels doing a handstand," says Justine McLucas, who moved her pole dancing school to Rochester Place in the summer of 2012 – in buildings which a century ago housed warehouses, coach and van builders and the like.

Justine's old studio was in a west London warehouse knocked down to make way for top-end flats. But the move has been a boost for the school. "I've found that business thrives much better in this area – maybe the clientele of Camden are just a little more open to this kind of recreation."

What kind, exactly? Justine herself was a professional ballerina and then spent nine years as an investment banker before setting up her own studio. She says that several of her instructors are also City types.

And those who come to the classes? Well, both women and men, from students to over fifties. And no, you don't have to wear heels.

"Dance is more fun than the gym," says Justine, "and pole dancing is so rewarding. Getting that crazy trick or invert right really makes you feel amazing. It's empowering. We do run sexy workshops and twerking and all that – but my main focus is on contemporary dance and on the gymnastic side of pole."

And the École de Pole has developed a particular specialism – a lot of circus performers come to train. The old beams and trussing of what was apparently a textiles warehouse have been reinforced to take the rigging of circus equipment including aerial hoops and poles. Classes cover skills including contortion and extreme stretching. Not often you come across that on a school curriculum.

29 | EELS, PIE AND MASH

Tucked away on Royal College Street lies what is probably Camden's oldest restaurant. That, at any rate, is the claim of Fred Howell, whose family have run the place for more than eighty years. In all that time they have served up what was once a London staple, eel and mash – and they still do.

In the warm, rather steamy restaurant the lunch-time crowd is tucking into this wholesome fare. It's remarkably cheap for a central London establishment. Eel and mash is the most pricy, at £4.80; jellied eels is a snip at £3.30; and there is the popular pie and mash at £3.50. All to be followed with traditional favourites such as spotted dick, treacle pudding or jam sponge (with or without custard) at a mere £1.90.

No wonder the room is full to bursting!

We caught up with Dave Smith, a pensioner, as he was leaving the cafe. "I've been coming thirty years. Best eels in London!"

In the kitchen Fred, now a spry 71, is peeling potatoes for tomorrow's lunch – the only time of day they are open.

Fred's cousin, Ray Castle, opened the restaurant on the other side of the street in 1934. But Ray's wife, Lil, soon took it over and decided that the western side of Royal College Street was infinitely superior and moved premises. "I have no idea why," says Fred. But here it has remained all these years.

Fred now only works part-time – leaving most of the hard graft to his son, Grant, who is kneading the dough for tomorrow's pies.

Once all the eels would have come from the Thames – but pollution killed them off. By 1878, British Freshwater Fishes reported that 'the eel-fare… no longer exists, on account of the filthy water around London'.

In fact, Castle's sells no English eels at all. "They're rubbish now," says Fred, taking time off from his peeling. "Taste all earthy. English eels are finished."

All the eels he serves are purchased from Mick Jenrick who operates from Billingsgate market and Canning Town in Poplar. "He's the king of eels," says Fred and it is no idle boast.

Mick has been dealing in eels at Billingsgate since the 1960s and around 40% of all the eels passing through the UK market are sold by his firm. This is up to seven tonnes a week, the bulk of which is processed into jelly in Mick's own factory.

Eels have been a staple at Billingsgate since the 17th century, when Dutch eel fishermen, whose boats were moored on the Thames, helped feed the people of London during the Great Fire and in exchange were granted a monopoly on eel trading at the market. Most of the eels still come from the Netherlands, though some are from Lough Neagh in Northern Ireland, home to Europe's biggest commercial wild eel fishery.

The title of London's oldest eel and pie shop belongs to M. Manze, whose shop in Peckham opened in 1902. At the end of the Second World War there were around a hundred such establishments. Most have since closed.

But judging by the enthusiasm of its customers, Castle's Pie and Mash has a bright future.

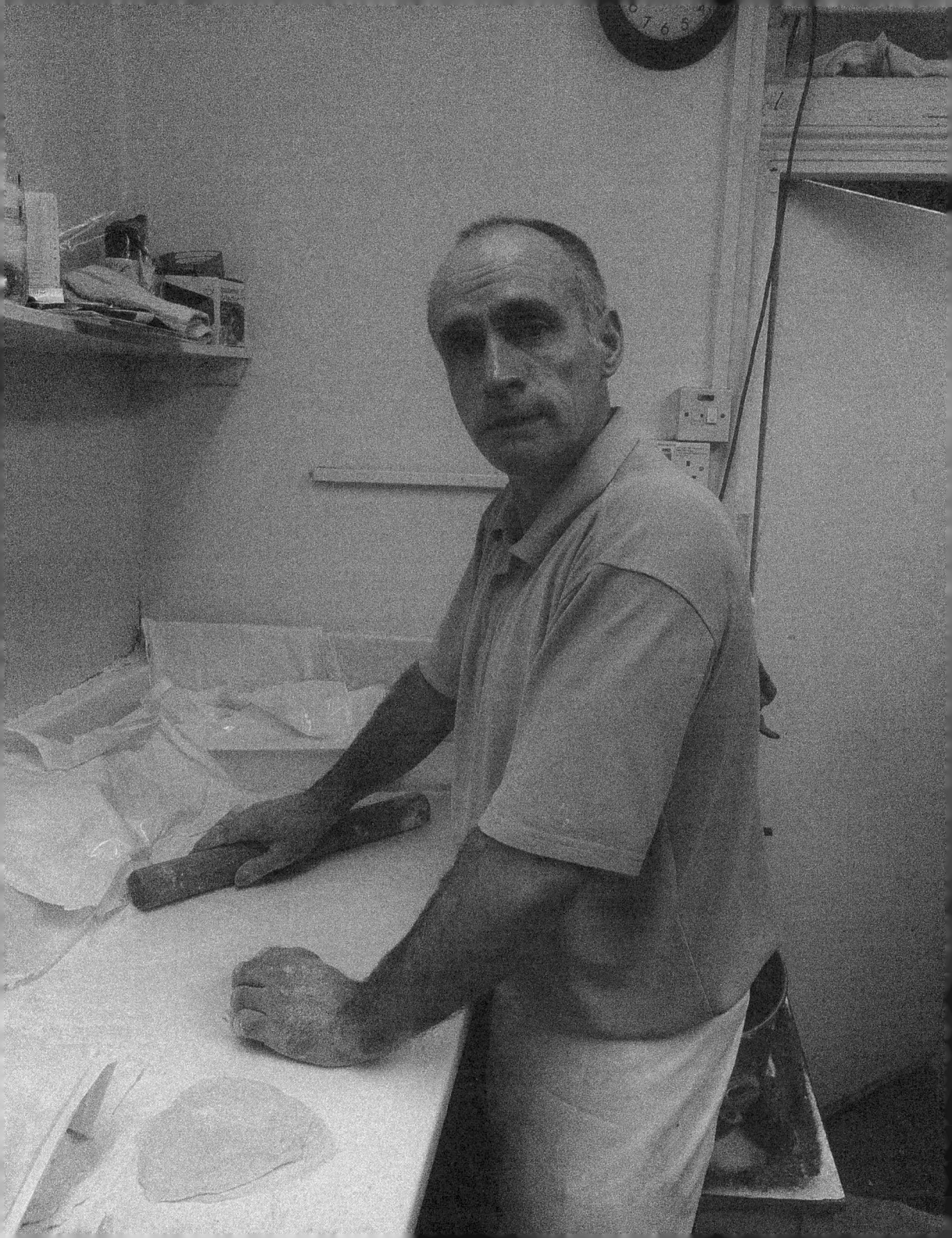

ACKNOWLEDGEMENTS

Brian Kelly, a distinguished freelance cameraman and long-standing Camden resident, has given of his time and skill to take half-a-dozen or so of the more memorable photos in *Curious Camden Town*. We are grateful.

Adam Ritchie has given permission to include his marvellous photo 'Sparklerman', taken on the night of the *International Times* launch at the Roundhouse. The archive photograph of the Regent's Park Barracks by Christina Broom is courtesy of the Museum of London. The photograph of young Morris dancers in Cumberland Market is included by kind permission of Getty Images. Robert Bevan's 'Cumberland Market, North Side' is courtesy of Southampton City Art Gallery and Bridgeman Images.

Nancy Edwards designed the map which graced *Curious Kentish Town* and has again been our splendid cartographer for this publication. Her own website is at www.nancyedwards.co.uk.

Chris Matthews has in his design given an ample measure of dash and distinction to *Curious Camden Town*. Ross Bradshaw of Five Leaves, our publisher, has shown huge confidence in our Curious idea – we hope we have lived up to his expectations.

Across Camden Town, we have been welcomed into homes, shops, workplaces, allotments and churches with universal generosity and hospitality, and many more have shared memories and information which have shaped this book. Thank you! And a particular word of appreciation for Tudor Allen and his colleagues at the Camden Local Studies and Archives Centre at Holborn Library, which plays such a vital role in recording and promoting awareness of Camden's history.